PWAC Guide to

Roughing it in the Market:

PWAC Guide to

Roughing it in the Market:

A Survival Toolkit for the Savvy Writer

Angie Gallop

Periodical
Writers
Association
of Canada

Support for this project has been provided by the Human Resources Initiative Program, an initiative of Cultural Careers Council Ontario and Human Resources Development Canada. PWAC also acknowledges the ongoing support of the Canada Council for the Arts and Ontario Ministry of Culture.

Editors: Liz Warwick and Trudy Kelly Forsythe
Copy editor/indexer: Ruth Bradley-St-Cyr
Production Coordinator: Susan Stevenson
Graphic Design: someone.ca
Printing & Binding: Coach House Printing

Published by:
Periodical Writers Association of Canada (PWAC)
National Office
54 Wolseley St. Suite 203
Toronto, Ontario, M5T 1A5
Tel: (416) 504-1645
Fax: (416) 504-9079
PWAC Web Site: *www.pwac.ca*
Find a Professional Writer: *www.writers.ca*

National Library of Canada Cataloguing in Publication

Gallop, Angie, 1972-
    PWAC guide to roughing it in the market: a survival toolkit for the savvy writer / Angie Gallop.

Includes index.
ISBN 0-9694028-1-3

    1. Authorship--Marketing. I. Periodical Writers Association of Canada. II. Title.

PN161.G34 2003   808'.02   C2003-903862-9

Contents

Acknowledgements

This project has been an incredible learning experience and I
want to thank all of the people mentioned in the book who so
freely shared their experiences, tips, and written pieces about
how to survive and even thrive while living the writing life (see
bios at the end of this book).

In particular, I want to thank Liz Warwick, who volunteered her
patience, enthusiasm, and time to edit the manuscript and guide
the project. Trudy Kelly Forsythe also reviewed and edited the
manuscript, without pay, alongside the challenge of being a new
mom. Ruth Bradley-St-Cyr copy edited the text and produced the
index. Aaron Benson and Oliver Barnett at someone.ca designed
the book and patiently stuck with us through many revisions.
Gordon Graham stepped in at a critical time to help me organize
my notes, my thoughts, myself, to get a workable outline and the
writing underway. Also, to Sheelagh Matthews, Denyse O'Leary,
and Christine Peets who volunteered their time to hire a writer
for this project and who expressed their faith in me. I also want
to thank PWAC Executive Director Susan Stevenson who very
patiently acted as project manager, and found the funding for this
project from the Human Resources Initiatives Program (an
initiative of Cultural Careers Council Ontario and Human
Resources Development Canada). And finally, I want to thank the
PWAC National Executive, a group of incredibly dedicated
volunteers who continue to fuel and drive an eclectic, very
functionally democratic, and fun organization of which I am
proud to be a member.

Angie Gallop
Montreal
June 2003

Introduction

This is not a book about the writer's life or process.* This is a book about the savvy it takes to make a decent living as a writer. Strategy and good business practices are not just the domain of people in stuffy suits. They form the foundation on which writing dreams become reality. Smart writers have a plan, know how to ask for the money they deserve and understand contracts so that they don't sell themselves short. Consider this book a boot camp of sorts. Its mission: To put you through some basic training so you can work for yourself in style.

Collected in these pages are some of the business wisdom basics and practical tools shared among members of the Periodical Writers Association of Canada (PWAC). Throughout the book we've also included some snippets of the advice that members exchange on a daily basis over the association's internal listserv, affectionately known as the "L." It all comes from years and years of experience as these writers have learned the hard way about what works and what doesn't when dealing with the publishing market.

This book also has a political purpose of sorts. Writers who work together to demand their rights and educate each other ensure Canadian publications continue to flourish with fresh ideas, insight, and stories worthy of sharing on an international scale.

PWAC was founded in 1976 when a group of writers got together to organize for industry-wide standard contracts and professional conduct. PWAC co-founder Heather Robertson says the most important thing in those days was the sense of community.

It still is.

Today, more than 500 writers across Canada support each other daily with professional (and sometimes personal) advice and the inside scoop on markets through PWAC. This collection of artistic entrepreneurs has expertise on every topic imaginable and sinks thousands of volunteer hours (not to mention wicked creativity) into lobbying for writers' rights as well as creating services and professional development opportunities for writers.

With this book, we hope to share a slice of the dynamism that results when writers work together to deal with the practical challenges inherent in the writing life.

* For an excellent book on the writer's life and process see The Write Track: How to Succeed as a Freelance Writer in Canada by Betty Jane Wylie.

Chapter 1

Savvy Writers Strategize

The first step in creating a writing business that will sustain you with work you enjoy is to stop writing. We freelancers too easily get caught up in our deadlines. Many among us seldom stop our work to step back and plan. So now is the time. Take your hands off the keyboard. Put down that pen. Put on your CEO shoes and take a look at your freelance-writing business.

And yes. If you are not yet in touch with that reality, or would rather that it just go away, well then that is your first step: To realize freelance writing is a business.

Do the Math

A bohemian lifestyle is not the prerequisite for great work. You can take risks to get your stories and hang out in an attic while you write them. But when it comes to selling your work, a business-like approach is what it takes to create the foundation you need to develop your passion for the act of writing. Many writers undervalue their work so while the people who sell the ads, print the publication or clean up the offices have all seen their wages keep pace with the cost of living, writers' rates have stagnated and even declined during the past 30 years.

Meanwhile, costs have dramatically increased. Gone are the days when a typewriter, answering machine, tape recorder, a good relationship at the post office and, maybe, a camera, were the standard office requirements for writers. Today's home office can't function without a much more costly computer, fax machine, and Internet access. And that optional camera? It's gone digital. That isn't the end of it. With the dawning of electronic communications and the concentration of media ownership, publishers are asking for, and getting, more secondary copyrights from writers than ever before.

The first step in reversing this trend is for you, as a writer, to become vigilant in knowing how much money you need to be asking for to support yourself. So, before you start on that next writing assignment, do the math. Let's say you want to earn $40,000 per year. Start with 365 days (approximately 52 weeks). If you don't want to work on the weekend (I don't recommend it!), subtract 104 days = 261. If you take a two-week break over the winter-holiday season, subtract another 14 days = 247 days. If you want a two-week summer break, subtract another 14 days = 233 days. Of course there are those fabulous long-weekends, so subtract another seven days = 226. With these calculations, you have about 45 weeks to work each year.

Now, it would be great if you could work for 45 weeks, five days each week, eight hours each day and be paid for it. Freelancing is not that simple. Especially when you are first starting out, a lot of your time is spent on marketing, paperwork, office clean-up,

Finance Tips for Freelancers

Twenty years ago, accountant Amanda Mills, was asked to manage a theatre company so far in debt that cash flow was a daily concern. After this trial by fire, she founded Artbooks – a firm dedicated exclusively to financial management in the arts. She and Toronto Star personal finance columnist Ellen Roseman, who works as a freelancer from time to time, offer some tips to help increase your financial confidence:

• **Keep track of every penny you spend:**
Write notes on the backs of your receipts or keep a small notepad handy. This will help you understand how your spending habits affect your financial health and budget more accurately and effectively.

• **Budget time to scrutinize all bills and statements, and negotiate:**
Negotiating works. When Roseman called her credit card company to cancel her card, it offered her an eight percent

filing, networking, and strategy. So, instead of figuring in 40 billable hours each week, cut that in half = 20. Multiply 20 hours by 45 weeks and you have about 900 billable hours each year to earn your income. If you want that income to be $40,000, (divide 40,000 by 900) you need to be making about $45 an hour.

But again, unfortunately, it is not quite that simple. Freelancers pay their own taxes, insurance, benefits, and many of their expenses. So to clear $40,000 per year, you need to be making at least $50 per hour.

Now, let's take a look at what most publications are offering these days. Many people say the industry standard rate is $1 per word. Unfortunately, the reality is many trade magazines and newspapers pay less than 50 cents per word. Many general interest magazines also pay about 50 cents a word while the glossy magazines pay a buck a word. There are some exceptions with high-end publications paying more to specific writers. At the time of writing this book, a couple of new Canadian

---

interest rate decrease. Call your hydro, phone, Internet providers, and any other suppliers to discuss ways to reduce those rates.

• **Disability insurance:**
Get some. If something happens and you can't work, those bills will still come in the mail.

• **Check your credit rating:**
There is a new service – www.equifax.ca – where you can get a report of how you rate and how to improve your rating.

• **Put aside money for an RRSP no matter what your debt load:**
Debts are important but you only save that 10-18 percent interest by paying them off. When you put the money into an RRSP, you can write it off against your income plus you will earn interest. Plus, it is critical to take care of yourself by diverting some of that hard-earned cash into your own coffers.

• **Save all of your personal receipts as well as your business receipts:**
Mills says there are more audits happening than ever before. One way to prove the receipts you are claiming are legitimate is to show the receipts you are not claiming. Err on the side of more

magazines were promising higher rates – but these assignments are the exception for most writers.

So, for this calculation's sake, let's say you write 50 articles (a little more than an article per week) at about 1000 words each (50,000 words) and that you'll earn an average of 50 cents per word. You'd have an income of $25,000 per year – before you start paying your taxes and expenses.

Life is not as cut and dried as "doing the math" portrays. But what it illustrates is that newspaper and magazine rates do not alone provide a living for the majority of freelancers. Later on, we'll talk about creating a mix of work so you can get some creative satisfaction and still pay those bills.

The Good News

Good writing is still very valuable and there are many writers out there who make a good living. The collective experience of PWAC is that adversity breeds creativity. As PWAC member Barbara Florio Graham said in a recent speech, "Writers are among the

deductions because auditors look to take away expense claims. The guiding principle to write-offs is "Can I prove it?" Mills, for example, has her actor clients create two closets – one for personal clothing and one for work-related clothing.

• **Get a GST number and sign up for the Quick Method:**
All businesses that make over $30,000 are required to have a GST number. Not having one indicates to clients that you make under $30,000. With a GST number, you are responsible to collect goods and service taxes from your clients and remit them to the government. Although having a GST number adds headaches, many freelancers choose to calculate and remit the taxes using the Quick Method of accounting. This makes it much easier and the percentage that the method assumes for expenses is generally favourable for writers. You can register for a GST number online at *www.businessregistration.gc.ca.*

• **Consider paying off your taxes before your credit card:**
Mills admits this is controversial. Credit cards have higher interest rates, but you can see that trip to Mexico or new pair of boots on

most versatile of the self-employed business owners." In a typical week, "it's not uncommon for someone who earns his primary living from writing and editing to do the desktop publishing of a brochure for a client, take photographs for a travel article, teach a continuing education class, work on a novel, and submit several poems to a competition."

Creativity in terms of the services you offer, how you market them, and how you get the stories you are burning to tell out into the world are all a part of the strategy you put together when you step into the role of CEO of your writing business.

Make a Plan

Tracey Arial, author of three books and a former national president of PWAC, does a long-term plan every five years and a shorter-term annual plan. She says the process is well worth the time. Looking back on her various plans, Arial says she sees a real power in defining her goals, even though life has never unfolded the way she expected. "Identifying where I wanted to go is what

---

the bill. "Tax bills tend to overwhelm and depress people," she says. Mills has seen people become visibly more relaxed, clear about money, and able to focus on their work once they start to plan for tax payments by automatically deducting GST and income taxes from their cheques.

• **Work your budget forecasts around your regular income:**
Mills says artists tend to perceive low cash times as "crises," and times when they have cash as "normal." Shift this perception and build your budget around the low cash times. Put any surplus aside to create a cushion

that is at least three times your monthly budget. This cushion will give you the confidence you need to become more prosperous.

• **Remember your energy follows your expectations:**
Sound money management is a skill and like any other, it takes practice and confidence. Getting your financial house in order and developing an ability to talk openly about money will reduce stress and increase your focus on what must get done. If you are confident about your ability to be financially successful, you will more likely achieve it.

has made a difference," she says. "Looking back, I'm astonished to see that although I hadn't looked at my five-year plan for a long time, I clearly have been directing myself toward my goals."

Arial says it's important that her plans include all spheres of her life – work, family, health, and friends – so she can see how they interconnect. By writing down her goals and how to achieve them, she avoids feeling overwhelmed. Once her plans are down on paper, she can put them out of her mind and get on with her work. She says this focus has helped the quality of her relationships with her clients. "I think I'm able to concentrate on my client relationships better because I've already reviewed for myself how working with each of them fits with my overall goals," she says.

Here are some basic tools to help you create and refine a strategy for yourself. They won't yield a professional business plan ready for investor scrutiny. Instead, they are aimed at helping you clarify your vision so you can focus your creative and marketing energies. Do as little or as much of this process as you wish and adapt it to fit your needs. Just be sure that you are putting some time aside to step into those CEO shoes and take a business perspective on how your writing fits with the rest of your life, not only as a dream but as a viable income source.

Tool 1: Set Your Priorities

Take a blank page and list your goals, your projects (both dream projects and money projects), your family obligations, and your physical routine – everything that takes up time in your week:

1. Novel

2. Monthly newsletter

3. Brochures for Flummex Corporation

4. Feature articles

5. Teaching

6. Advertorial work

7. Yoga

8. Triathlon training

9. Time with family

10. Time with friends

Now, take a long view, think of your lifetime, and go down your list and compare #1 to #2 – which is more important? Put a point beside the priority that is most important. Then compare #1 to #3 through #6, putting a point beside the priority that is the most important. Then start with #2 and compare it to #3 through #6. Continue your way down the list. When you are finished, tally up the score for each item. While this process may seem complicated, it forces you to isolate the different spheres of activity in your life and examine objectively how each relates to your other priorities.

Now, think of this year and what you have to accomplish in the short term. Make a new list and do the comparison exercise again. This will help you create a picture of where you are right now, and where you want to be in the long term.

From the "L": Kathe Lieber on the Freelancer's Mantra — Work Smarter, Not Harder

The key to keeping food in the fridge and a roof over your head is having a mixture of "bread-and-butter" clients and "jam" clients. The bread-and-butter variety are the ones who count on you, which means you can (usually) count on them. Save their bacon once or twice and they'll go down the hall to accounting and scream when your cheque is late. They will tell their colleagues, friends, and family how wonderful you are and circulate your contact information. In short, they are pleasant, professional, and pay promptly – the three "Ps" in my book.

"Jam" clients are great in a different way. You get the opportunity to learn – and learning is one of the best parts of freelancing, n'est-ce pas? The jam projects tend to be intense and may involve unreasonable deadlines but when it's going well, you are soaring on an incredible high. Alas, you may crash afterward when the cheque takes months to arrive.

So how do you get a mix that keeps you sane and solvent? Here

Tool 2: Predict Your Income

Take a sheet of paper and make a column for each month of the year that you plan to work. Then create rows for each service you plan to sell or revenue source you expect this year. Then, working quickly, predict how much money you think you can make from each source. When you are finished, tally up the totals for each month. Then tally up the total income you predict you will make for the year. Don't worry about making your predictions perfect. These earning goals for each month add some urgency to your work and help you focus.

Tool 3: Make it Real – Practical Steps and Deadlines

Take your list of priorities and create a list of practical steps for yourself over the next year to advance your priorities. Attach deadline dates to each item. Put these into your calendar.

---

are a few pointers I've learned from 20/20 hindsight:

• **Get some sort of regular gig:**
A column, a newsletter – if you have a couple of these on your roster you won't starve. Your main asset here is your complete reliability. You may even be able to negotiate a retainer, which will give you what every freelancer dreams of: A modicum of financial stability.

• **Develop a sideline:**
I translate (French to English) and edit as well as writing. For some of my clients, I do all three.

• **Nurture your regulars:**
Invite your favourite client to lunch now and then. (Chances are they'll pick up the tab!) Send them clippings you think might be of interest. Pick their brains occasionally – most people love to be regarded as information sources. If you haven't heard from one of your regulars in a while, call up to check in. I've had clients who moved to bigger and better things and took me with them, partly because I kept in touch.

• **Follow up assiduously:**
If Montreal PWACer Stephanie Whittaker doesn't hear back

Sample List of Practical Steps for Feature Articles

1. *Study four new glossy magazines in my interest area per month. Short report due Friday of each week.*

2. *Have "Secretary Security" piece ready for HR Professional Jan. 17*

3. *"Talking About Money" ready for Report on Business Feb. 15*

4. *Create a database to collect personal markets information March 30*

5. *Send out three queries per week based on available material. Due Monday, Wednesday, and Friday of each work week.*

6. *Develop one new original query per week. Due Friday of each week.*

You may also want to make a mission statement for yourself. This affirmation about the type of person and writer you want to be can help you clarify and re-focus when you feel bogged down. Again, don't worry about getting it perfect the first time. You can review and refine it with time.

from an editor within a day or two, she phones and says, "This is my quality control check-up. I'm calling to find out whether you're satisfied with the product I sent you." Most editors are "quite stunned," she reports.

• **If you can't do the job, suggest a reliable replacement:**
Work sharing pays off. When I'm super-busy and can't handle an assignment, I like to suggest a colleague. I make sure it's someone who can provide work of comparable quality to my own. Every time I've done this, the client has come back to me the next time.

• **Be realistic about your work habits:**
I work fast but I know my limits and keep a list of my current projects by my phone to check before I say "yes" to more work. Amazingly often, if the client tells me on Tuesday that she needs the job by the following Monday but I tell her I can't do it till Thursday, she'll decide that Thursday is okay. So take the time to take stock. Make your working hours really count. Working smarter can do wonders for your confidence and self-respect.

Sample Mission Statements

I increase the level of authenticity and joy in the world both through my writing and teaching and through my dealings with other people.

I pay my way in the world by telling stories that make a difference.

Next, think about the values that will help you achieve your mission.

Sample Values

1. *I act out of love and enthusiasm, not fear.*

2. *I work hard to push the articles I want to write into the world.*

3. *I am financially healthy.*

4. *I am physically, emotionally, and spiritually healthy.*

Now think of seven or eight very practical things you can do to incorporate your values into your business and daily life.

Sample List of Practical Steps for "I Am Financially Healthy"

1. *Put time aside for market research in targeted areas of interest.*

2. *Make a recycling plan and carry it out to use past research, themes, and ideas more effectively.*

3. *Focus volunteer energy to ensure it does not interfere with writing business.*

4. *Assess new clients to ensure they pay well enough.*

5. *Negotiate with editors who offer low pay.*

6. *Record and keep receipts when I spend money.*

7. *Update my accounts at least once each month and use this information to review my budget.*

8. *Do a monthly strategy session to assess how I'm doing financially and brainstorm creative ways to meet the challenges that crop up.*

Tool 4: Create a Budget

Use your projected income to make a budget. Don't forget to put aside the GST you collect, income tax, RRSP, and savings. Also, look into a disability and extended health benefits package and any additional insurance you need for office equipment. (Beware! Some home insurance policies don't cover computers if they are used for business.)

Try to be as accurate as you can: How many times a month do you pay that $1.50 charge for an ATM machine? What are your monthly bank service fees? How much are your credit card interest charges? How much do you plan to donate? Again, don't be obsessed about being perfect. Just get something down so that you have a basic spending guide. Track your spending and make adjustments accordingly.

Tool 5: Client Review

Turn the tables and take a look at what your clients are doing for you. Go through your files and make a list of all your clients/jobs/writing projects from the past couple of years. Create a table with four columns. In the first column put "Fun," in the second column put "Money," in the third column put "Learning" and finally put "Total Score" in the final column. Working quickly, go down the list and rate

---

Writing Across the Border

If you cultivate an American publication or client, you'll need to know about another important business number: The Individual Taxpayer Identification Number (ITIN). An ITIN allows you to be exempt from having US taxes withheld on your cheques. To apply, you need to fill out IRS form W-7. You can find it in the forms database at www.irs.gov. To apply, you'll have to supply a passport, driver's license, birth, or marriage certificate, baptism certificate, or school records. The IRS has authorized different accounting firms throughout the world to be ITIN acceptance agents. For a list of these firms in Canada, go to www.irs.gov and type "Acceptance Agents Canada" into the IRS site search engine.

Once you have your ITIN, fill out a W-8BEN form (also available from www.irs.gov) and provide a copy to each of your US publishers before they pay you. Publishers who don't receive it before issuing payment are required by US law to withhold 30 percent of your money for Uncle Sam's tax people, the Internal Revenue Service.

each client on a scale of one to three in each category. One is poor and three is excellent.

When you are finished, tally up the points for each client. This should give you an idea of who supports your goals the most. Take the top four clients and create a list of practical steps (with deadlines attached) to improve your relationship, generate more work, and draw on them to improve your business network. Think about the topic areas that you've enjoyed writing about and draw up a list of practical steps you can take to find new clients or publications in these areas.

Tool 6: Summarize

To help you take an objective look at yourself and your business, create a quick executive summary for your plan. You can use this summary to look back on and gauge your progress. Use the third person perspective and describe your current circumstances and your future goals. Use past tax returns, your income projection, and any other factual information you can provide to illustrate where you are now, where you are headed, how you plan to achieve your goals and the challenges you face along the way. Once you have a basic plan in place, record the deadlines in your calendar, and then put it away. Refer to it when you need to review prospective projects or to inspire yourself to carry out the more difficult tasks to reach your goals.

Tracey Arial says that for all the plans she has written, she has never followed even one of them to the letter. "Once I finish planning life takes over and I go from hectic day to hectic day," she says. "A business plan doesn't make life less hectic but it helps me to be inspired in all aspects of my life."

Chapter 2

Savvy Writers Negotiate

A plan for yourself and an idea of how you will manage the money you earn is one half of the equation. The other half is asking for, and getting paid properly for the work you do.

What is a Reasonable Rate?

In previous years, PWAC created fee guidelines based on information it collected from members across the country and from employers in the various industries that hire writers on a freelance or contract basis. What this research revealed is there is no simple answer. It all comes down to what you negotiate. Pay rates vary according to:

- The type of assignment (magazine article, corporate report, et cetera)
- Your skills and background
- The time the project will require for research, re-writes, and approvals
- The rights licensed
- Where you are located (i.e., urban markets, where the cost of living is higher, tend to be higher paying)

Writers – not to mention editors and other clients – disagree about pay rates. Writers regularly hear all kinds of arguments from clients who can't or won't pay them more. "We're just starting out. We don't have that kind of money," "Well, I have two other writers working for me and they don't charge that much…" As a result, writers sometimes undercut their own efforts by accepting low pay because they want to see their name in print or fear they'll never get better-paying work.

It's time to put a stop to this by remembering this rule: You'll only get what you ask for. Sure, the client may refuse, but at least you've made your point that good writing has value. The fee guidelines (see the "Freelance Writing Rates Scale" below) represent the reality in 2003, at the time of writing, but it's up to every writer to start demanding better, fairer pay. Use these fees as ballpark figures – then try to slam that ball out of the stadium with some negotiating savvy. As this book ages, check *www.writers.ca* for fee guideline updates.

Many writers, such as Hélèna Katz, track how many hours they spend researching and writing articles. When offered an

Freelance Writing Rates Scale

Periodical Writing
General Interest/Consumer Magazines
$1.00 to $2.00 per word
$500 to $10,000 per article
$400 to $1500 per column

Trade/Special Interest Magazines
$0.30 to $2.00 a word
$500 to $4000 per article
$300 to $1000 per column

Newspaper Writing
Large Daily Newspapers
$0.30 to $1.00 per word
$250 to $2500 per article
$330 to $1250 per column
Community Newspapers
$0.10 to $0.50 per word
$75 to $1000 per article
$75 to $500 per column

Web Writing
Varies widely, business sites pay more
$1.00 to $3.00 per word
$60 to $100 per hour

Advertising Material
Copy/Scripts/News Releases/Brochures
$350 to $500 per page
$750 to $1000 per project for brochures
$75 to $150 per hour

Advertorials
$75 to $150 per hour
Includes travel and think time, meetings, phone calls, and interviews

Corporate Writing
Reports/Marketing Plans/Technical Writing
$3.00 to $5.00 per word
$500 to $15,000
$75 to $150 per hour

assignment, Katz can quickly estimate how many hours it will take – and then evaluate if the price offered is acceptable. When she started out, Katz posted PWAC's fee guidelines on a wall by her desk to use as a quick reference so she could see how an offer compared to market rates.

Don't Agonize, Negotiate!

Freelance writers are not unionized in Canada so publishers can negotiate writer-by-writer, contract-by-contract. As media owners become part of huge corporate conglomerates, they are starting to create standard contracts that pay less and ask for more. In this

Editing
Varies according to publication/project
$50 to $100 per hour

Ghost Writing
Negotiable, based on the publishing and writing experience of the author/co-author/ghost
Articles:
Generally 2-3 times the writer's usual rate
Books:
$25,000 to $75,000 flat fee
Entire advance + 50% of royalties

Government Writing
News Releases/Studies/Reports
$2.00 to $5.00 per word
$3000 to $150,000 per project
$60 to $200 per hour

Newsletters
Writing only; layout extra
$1.00 to $2.00 per word
$400 to $8000 per issue
$75 to $150 per hour

Scripts
Radio (highly variable)
$75 to $150 per minute of script
Television (highly variable)
$100 to $150 per minute of script

Speech Writing
$1000 to $10,000 per speech
$100 to $150 per hour

Teaching/Instruction
Varies according to experience and subject
$30 to $150 per hour
$500 to $1000 per day

Translation/Adaptation
Literary: $0.50 to $1.00 per word
Other: $0.25 per word
$80 to $150 per hour

environment, it is becoming critical for freelance writers to study, practice, and master the art of negotiating reasonable rates for their work.

As Katz says, writers have to stop being thankful that editors are accepting their work and start seeing themselves as professionals who are running a business and offering a valuable service. "Negotiating can be terrifying at first and the only way to build confidence is to start doing it," she says. "I've found it gets easier." The key, according to Katz, is to not take refusals personally. Instead, treat them like the business decisions that they are. "I find that it makes things easier for me if I depersonalize the whole messy business. That way I don't take it as a reflection of my skills as a writer but rather as the editor's or client's ability to decide to pay for the quality work I provide."

Writers looking for work in the magazine and newspaper market are in a tougher negotiation position because so many writers are willing to write for little or no money, thus undercutting the market. Editors are usually not business people, they are editors, and often their superiors have told them that freelancers must sign a (usually not very writer-friendly) contract. They also have their fair share of pressure on their plates. As freelance writers, it's too much to ask an editor to look out for our interests, we have to be responsible for ourselves.

Knowledge is Power

How well informed you are during a negotiation is in direct proportion to the success of your outcome. Research the going rates and study the needs of the publication or organization you are pitching so you can be well versed during the conversation.

Tim Perrin, a freelancer and writing instructor who practiced as a lawyer for seven years, recommends that you also work the grapevine to find out as much as you can about the person with whom you are hoping to negotiate. Ask around for associate editors or writers who work with them. Then, take a good look at yourself and what you bring to the table. Remember, as Perrin says, the pressure is mutual. Magazine editors have to fill their publications with quality material on a budget that is, usually, too small. Book editors have to find and buy profitable books. So, price is not the only bargaining chip on the table. Reliability, quality, and an ability to deliver on short notice are all worth money once you can demonstrate them. A title, such as "author" helps, as does some expertise in your subject area. And, if you have exclusive access to a source or a photo, prepare yourself to go for the gold.

During negotiation, Perrin says you can continue your detective work by using open-ended questions. Be sure to clarify any terms you don't understand. Phrases such as: "I'm sorry, I'm not

From the "L": Mark Zuehlke on Making it Pay

Author Mark Zuehlke says writers should forget per word rates. Instead, they should calculate the per hour rate and give magazines what they've paid for. "Ignore the rates the magazines pay. Try instead to set an hourly rate for yourself and then confine the time you spend on an article to how many hours the fee will buy. So, if a magazine is paying you $200 for a piece and you have an hourly rate of $50, then the article is researched, written and invoiced in four hours. If you keep close to this policy, you'll earn what you are worth every time you put fingers to keyboard, regardless of the rates offered by the publications. The magazine, meanwhile, will still probably be getting more value than they are paying.

"About confidence and asking for more money, I think most writers never really have this confidence. Every single time I do it, I have to take a big gulp and then go for it and I've been freelancing full-time for 19 years. I have learned, however, that if you ask you will usually get some more money and continue to get work from the publication. And, should they refuse and you part ways – because I don't think you ask for a raise without the intention of walking if you don't get it – there is always more opportunity out there somewhere."

clear, can you tell me what you mean by..." come in handy. Also, repeat what you've heard using a phrase such as "So what I'm hearing is..." This encourages the other person to elaborate. If, during the negotiation, it becomes obvious that the budget really is tight, be creative. Barter for some ad space, a subscription, access to research resources, or a tax receipt if the organization is a charity.

Tim Perrin's Tips on the Art of Negotiating

Negotiation is a skill that you can improve with practice. Here are some gambits and techniques to keep in mind:

- Don't take it or leave it: When someone tells you that a contract is non-negotiable, ask your questions anyway. If you are businesslike in your requests, you will not drive them away.
- Never be the first to name a price: If you are wedged into a corner with the client asking, "How much do you charge?" throw it back into their court with an outrageous reply. "Well if it were up to me to set a price, I'd want $10-a-word! So what's your budget?" Alternative option: Be seriously ridiculous and make big demands. In this way you have started with a lot that you can "give away" as the negotiation progresses.
- Make a big deal of any concession that you give and get a counter-concession.
- Never say "yes" to a first offer: Instead, use the "Perrin Pause": "Oh (silence). I was thinking it would be more like (triple the price)." Perrin says that he guarantees that although the other party won't triple, or even double the price, those who can, will offer more.
- Be the reluctant seller: "Hmmm (silence) I really appreciate you calling but when did you want this? (listen to answer) I have to take a look at my time (silence)." What you are really saying is: Make it worth my while.

- Make it easy for the other party to accept: Never put them into a situation where they will lose face if they say "Yes." Look at the situation from their point of view and make it easy for them to agree.
- Make your offers flexible.
- Maintain creativity and openness: Never narrow the negotiation to one issue where someone has to lose. Brainstorm creative options you can offer so you have things to trade off.
- Remember the "call girl" principle: The value of a service diminishes rapidly after the services have been performed. Make sure the deal is cut before you do the work.
- Try to be the one who writes the contract: Don't be lazy! Their paperwork will be less favourable to you than your own. Many employers appreciate freelancers who take care of these details. Use PWAC's Letter of Agreement (p. 43) and Standard Freelance Publication Agreement as templates (Appendix A).

Always maintain the ability to walk away. Make it a priority to maintain a business that is sufficiently active so you can keep your integrity intact.

If You Hit a Deadlock

- Refer to a higher authority: Perrin says he knows one writer who has made her husband her business manager. When she

---

From the "L": Michael O'Reilly on Getting a Better Rate

Michael O'Reilly has significantly boosted his bottom line with a simple practice: Never accept the first offer. "I ask for at least fifty percent more than the first offer. On rare occasions, the editors say no – usually when they have no control over their budget. Most of the time, they are so stunned that a freelancer would actually stick up for his rights that they say yes right away. The others come back with a counter-offer that is better than the first. I figure I've increased my income by forty percent since instituting this practice."

hits a negotiation impasse, she can pause the process and consult a second opinion.

- "Let's set this point aside": As you settle more and more issues, everybody becomes more invested, and more willing to find a compromise. The trick here is to bring the item you set aside back onto the table in the middle of the negotiation. Don't let it be the last item that prevents you from reaching an agreement at the end.
- "Put it in writing and let me see it": Use this if you have most of the items agreed. As people put things down on paper, they often hammer out the side issues. This tactic takes the negotiation off of the table for the short term and moves things forward.
- Withdraw: Remember, always maintain the ability to walk away.

Disputes Happen

A good negotiation lays down the foundation for a successful project. But even when the relationship is a good one, unexpected disputes can arise. "Most people just think to ask about the submission date and payment when they are assigned a story but there is much more to a negotiation," says Bruce Wilson, chair of PWAC's mediation committee. The single most important thing writers can do to avoid disputes is to have a project checklist system in place (see Paul Lima's "Yes" Checklist and The Estimating Checklist on pages 32 and 33) that helps clarify all of the terms with the client up front.

Wilson advises writers to pay attention when contract terms make you feel uncomfortable. "Often when writers are new they won't question uncomfortable terms and they inevitably find themselves ripped off," says Wilson. "It builds self esteem to assert contract terms that create good working relationships." Follow up your negotiations with a letter of agreement, send it by e-mail, and ask for a response. Save the response e-mail so that if a dispute comes up, you can prove that your client received and read your letter before the dispute arose.

Most of the cases Wilson sees arise when publishers don't pay writers for their work or re-use the work without the writer's permission. Be wary of new publishers who don't have a stable funding base. And, when dealing with larger companies, talk with them about extra payment if they re-use your work. Many editors today assume they can reprint freelance pieces on a Web site or in a database without paying an extra fee. This is based on a practice that is creeping into the industry where publishers have been adding it to contracts and giving writers the choice to sign or take their work elsewhere. This amounts to an attempt by publishers to erode an industry standard that used to be "one time print rights for $1 per word." At the time of writing this book, there are three class action lawsuits over electronic rights underway in Canada.

Another area of law that you'll want to look at is libel. While it is obviously important for practicing journalists, libel and defamation can also pop up in the course of doing business. Wilson said he had one case where a person was angry with a publisher, badmouthed that publisher, and was hit with a defamation suit. He recommends *Libel in a Nutshell*, by lawyer Peter Downard, which you can download in PDF form from *www.fasken-martineau.com*.

Checklists: The First Step in Avoiding Disputes

To help his negotiations go smoothly, PWAC member Paul Lima has developed two checklists. Use the first when an editor says "Yes" to an article and use the second when a client asks you for a cost estimate. These checklists on pages 32 and 33 will help you make sure to ask the right questions up front and have a clear picture of your assignments before you start.

Paul Lima's "Yes" Checklist

Keep this checklist handy to help you discuss/negotiate the details when an editor says "Yes" to one of your article query ideas:

1. Angle or central idea of the main article: What does the editor want?

2. Style: Does the publication use "centre" or "center"? Ask which style guide they use or request one if the publication has created its own style guide.

3. Contacts for research/interviews: Is there anyone in particular the editor wants you to contact?

4. Word count: How long do they want the piece to be?

5. Sidebar(s): Any chance you can add one if a particularly juicy piece of research comes up?

6. Due date: When do they want it?

7. Fact checking/contact list: Will you be doing the fact checking or will someone at the publication do it? Should you provide a contact list with the name, address, phone number, and e-mail of everyone you interviewed for the article?

8. Photography/illustrations: How will this work? Is the publication open to buying your photos? Does the editor want you to keep an eye out for photo possibilities?

9. Method of filing: What works best for the editor? E-mail? Imbedded in the main message or as an attached file?

10. Fee: How much are they paying?

11. Rights sought:
a) First print: local, regional, national
b) Electronic (web, database)
c) Translation

12. Contract or confirmation letter: Who will provide it?

13. Invoice: When and who?

14. Payment: When?
a) Upon receipt
b) Upon acceptance
c) Upon publication
d) X days after publication

15. Kill fee: Under what circumstances does the publication issue kill fees? What is the amount?

16. What if:
a) You have less/more of a story than discussed?
b) A contact is not co-operative?
c) You need a deadline extension?

Paul Lima's Estimating Checklist

Most clients are interested in their bottom line: "What is this project (article, press release, brochure, web page, speech, script...) going to cost me? What is your quote for this job?" Before you answer, you need to define what I call the boundaries of the box. To do this, you need information. Here are some questions you can ask:

- When does the project start?
- When is it due?
- What exactly am I expected to produce (known as the deliverables)?
- Who is the target audience?
- What impression do you want to leave them with? What action do you want them to take?
- Who will I work with as the primary point person?
- Will there be meetings to discuss this project? If so, how many, how long and where will they be held?
- How many people will I have to interview? By phone or in person?
- What kind of/ volume of background research do you expect me to conduct? What other research is required?
- What is the approval process? Who shuffles the document through the approval process?
- Do you need soft (files) and/or hard copy (paper)?

- What file format(s) do you need them in?
- Who takes it to the next step (design, printing, distribution, media contact, follow-up, video production...)?
- Will I be working with that person?

Take notes (get a headset or speaker phone!). When the client asks you for a quote on the spot, reply with "When do you need the estimate?" In other words, don't quote right away based on the conversation. Take an hour. Take twenty-four hours. Think it through. Then get back to the client with the quote based on how many hours you believe you will spend on the job times your hourly rate. Conclude your quote with: "This is based on the details we discussed. Any additional work, writing, meetings, revisions, interviews beyond what we discussed will be extra. I will advise you if I feel the work has moved beyond the scope of the job as we have defined it."

If you deliver your quote verbally, make sure you follow up with an e-mail or fax so it is in writing. The client may also want to send you a contract or purchase order that outlines the details of the project. Review it and make sure it conforms to what you understand to be the scope of the project.

After the negotiation is over, document all interactions with the editor or client throughout the project. Take notes, with dates and times, during telephone conversations or, better yet, tape the conversations. Wilson says he divides his project files into two parts: Research and business. In the business section, he keeps all contracts, e-mails, conversation notes, faxes, and all other correspondence about the project. "When a member comes to me asking for mediation assistance, I ask them to send me everything they have: A chronology of the events, e-mails, contracts and any other evidence of the interaction," he says. "When we go to an editor and show them the paper trail we often get results right away."

With good documentation, you can present the facts, rather than getting caught up in accusations. Time and time again, Wilson says he sees people fail to negotiate a settlement because they took a nasty approach. What often happens, he says, is the publisher serves the writer with a lawyer's letter. This makes it hard to fix the situation and negotiate a settlement person to person.

"My philosophy is to never base an argument on emotions. Instead, present people with the facts. The more respect you use to deliver your case, the more people will listen."

How to Take 'Em to Small Claims Court

If you've exhausted your avenues of mediation, you may decide to bring the dispute to a judge in small claims court.

Small claims court takes a lot of time and energy and it's up to you to educate yourself. If you have questions, talk to a lawyer about your specific case. Most law societies offer a lawyer referral service in each province and territory that is about $10 for a half hour. If you live in a city with a law school, you may be able to get help from a student law clinic. If you go to see a lawyer, gather your paperwork together – timeline, correspondence, et cetera, and send it in before your appointment in order to use your time in the lawyer's office efficiently. Alternatively, Self Counsel Press publishes a book about handling small claims cases that covers most of Canada – see *www.self-counselpress.com*.

The procedures and administrative costs vary widely across the country but generally you can sue in small claims court for failure to pay for services rendered; failure to fulfill the terms of a written or oral contract, and copyright infringements. Actions for libel and slander are not allowed. Small claims court does limit the amount of money you can claim for damages. The limits vary from province to province – anywhere from $3000 to $25,000.

If your problem is complex, you can bring a lawyer or a law student in some provinces. Other provinces actively discourage people from using lawyers in small claims court. Lawyer's fees are not awarded as part of court costs. Some provinces stipulate that the defendant must live in the province. Others have a mandatory mediation session conducted by a provincial court judge who will not be hearing your case. If the judge can't get a settlement then she can make pre-trial discovery orders, which essentially dictate who has to produce which documents when.

Before you file a claim, talk to people who have been through the process and attend a small claims court proceeding to familiarize yourself with the process. There are alternate ways to proceed. Outfits such as *www.sueonline.net* will do the legwork for you for a fee. Buyer beware: Before working with any contract agency find out exactly what you are paying for and how much money all of the steps of the process will cost.

For specific information, see the list of links on page 36 for small claims resources in your province or territory.

Small Claims Courts by Province

British Columbia (Small Claims Court: $10,000 limit)
Dispute Resolution Office: www.ag.gov.bc.ca/dro/

Small Claims Court:
www.ag.gov.bc.ca/courts/civil/smallclaims/index.htm
www.provincialcourt.bc.ca/quicklinks/smallclaimsmattersusefullinks.html
www.provincialcourt.bc.ca/aboutthecourt/smallclaimsmatters/index.html
www.provincialcourt.bc.ca/downloads/pdf/smallclaimsarticle93.pdf

Alberta (Provincial Civil Court: $25,000 limit)
www.albertacourts.ab.ca/pc/civil/publication/index.htm
www.albertacourts.ab.ca/pc/civil/forms/index.htm
www4.gov.ab.ca/just/lawu/court.cfm#ORG020

Saskatchewan (Small Claims Court: $5000 limit)
www.saskjustice.gov.sk.ca/courts/provcourt/small_claims/toc.shtml
www.plea.org/freepubs/scc/scc.PDF

Manitoba (Court of Queen's Bench: $7500 limit)
www.manitobacourts.mb.ca/SmallClaims.htm
web2.gov.mb.ca/laws/statutes/ccsm/c285e.php

Ontario (Small Claims Court: $10,000 limit)
www.attorneygeneral.jus.gov.on.ca/html/cad/sccbook.htm
www.fleurcom.on.ca/html/memo06.html

Quebec (Small Claims Division: $7000)
www.justice.gouv.qc.ca/english/publications/generale/creance-a.htm

New Brunswick (Small Claims Court: $6000 limit)
www.gnb.ca/acts/acts/s-09-1.htm

PEI (Supreme Court: Small Claims: $8000)
www.gnb.ca/acts/acts/s-09-1.htm
www.gov.pe.ca/courts/supreme/rules/

Nova Scotia (Small Claims Court: $10,000)
www.gov.ns.ca/just/small.htm
www.gov.ns.ca/just/regulations/regs/sccfrmpr.htm

Newfoundland & Labrador (Small Claims Court: $3000)
www.gov.nf.ca/just/provincial_court/publications/small_claims_procedures.htm
www.gov.nf.ca/just/provincial_court/publications/small%20claims%20rules.htm
www.gov.nf.ca/just/provincial_court/small_claims_court_forms.htm
www.gov.nf.ca/just/provincial_court/publications/small-claims.htm>

Chapter 3

Savvy Writers Know Their Rights

You own the copyright to what you write. Your copyright has value. It allows you to protect your work and make money by licensing it to a publisher or company. Whether you write for traditional print publications or new electronic media, a good understanding of how copyright works will help you to earn more money or explain why you aren't earning enough. The Canadian Copyright Act – which you can find at laws.justice.gc.ca/en/C-42 – contains everything that you need to know. The most important section, from a writer's point of view, is Section 13 (1), which says "...the author of a work shall be the first owner of the copyright therein." Simply put, once you write something down, you own it. Copyright comes into existence from the moment that a work is created. You don't have to register it, publish it, or even intend it for publication.

One point of confusion for many writers is the fact that ideas themselves aren't copyrightable. You may want to write an article about yoga injuries. If you tell your friend about it, you can't prevent him from taking that idea and writing his own story about it. What you can do is write the piece. When you write an idea down, what is copyrighted is the way you "fix" that idea into words.

A second important section is one that allows you to license your work to someone else for publication. Section 13 (4) says, "The owner of the copyright in any work may assign the right, either wholly or partially, and either generally or subject to limitations relating to territory, medium or sector of the market or other limitations relating to the scope of the assignment, and either for the whole term of the copyright or for any other part thereof, and may grant any interest in the right by licence, but no assignment or grant is valid unless it is in writing signed by the owner of the right in respect of which the assignment or grant is made, or by the owner's duly authorized agent."

That's right. You are in control of your copyright. Unless you sign it away. Careful management of copyright licences is key to making a living as a freelance writer. So, it is critical to understand your rights.

Copyright Basics

Copyright gives you the right to determine how others use your writing and for how much. The best way to derive the most benefit from copyright is to license one piece of your work to many non-competing publishers. While there is only one copyright in any given work, that copyright may be divided into many different rights. When you license your work to any publisher, a contract or letter of agreement is used to spell out the details.

Some clients write contracts that, when signed, mean you automatically assign or transfer all copyright to them. The federal and provincial governments normally assume all copyright ownership of material written for them, although it is possible to negotiate individual deals. Corporate clients often want all copyright as well. If you agree to relinquish all copyrights for a

---

From the "L": Why Should That Bother You?

Suzanne Boles: I'm starting to wonder if I am one of the first to get this contract and why it bothers me so much when I see that publishers are asking for the right to resell work without compensation to the writer?

Reply from Kevin Yarr: Why should that bother you? Just the other day I rented a car and then sold it. I thought about sharing the revenue with Avis, but the paperwork was so complicated. Of course, Avis was very understanding.

written work, you should be paid accordingly, because you will no longer be able to earn money from resale. If you're a staff writer, your employer usually owns your copyright, although this too is open to individual negotiation. If you work on staff at a magazine or newspaper that owns your copyright, you still retain the right to restrain your employer from publishing a specific piece.

If you want to make the most of your copyright, resist selling all rights to your work. Even when you wish to license many copyrights at the same time, resist lumping them together in a blanket contract. Negotiate each copyright independently to ensure that your clients pay individually for each one.

Print Rights

Print copyrights can be divided into two basic types – sequential and geographic. Sequential copyrights include first and second rights. A "first right" means that your client is licensing the right to publish a story first – something that's very important to some publishers. A "second right" covers any publication after the first time. Geographic copyrights limit the publication of a work to a specific area and usually only apply to a "first right." Geographic rights can expand as far as "galactic rights" or be specific to an individual city. Usually, a geographic right limits publication to a continent or within a country. You could sell the same story to three different publishers by licensing "first Canadian rights," "first US rights," and "first European rights."

It was once common to license serial rights, but this practice should now be avoided. A serial right traditionally covered the right to publish in a periodical or "serial" publication, but the word "serial" has come under legal scrutiny with the advent of electronic publishing. Some publishers argue that serial rights expand beyond print publication and include electronic database or World Wide Web rights. This question is currently before the courts. To avoid confusion, specify, "print rights only."

In some instances, particularly when assigning second rights, it is better to use language that avoids questions of geography and first or second rights. In this case, you could simply license "one-time print rights." This licence grants the publisher the right to use your work once, only in print. This way, you can sell the same article to a number of newspapers simultaneously, just as a syndicated columnist does, or perhaps sell second rights without explaining where the work has previously appeared. Be aware that it is unethical to license rights to the same story to publications who compete for the same readers.

Electronic Rights

Writers deserve to earn a fair return for their work, no matter how it is used. Publishers often complain that they're making no money from electronic publishing. Even though this assertion is highly debatable, it has no bearing on the agreement with you. These same publishers pay for the computer, Web designers, Internet space, CD-ROM production, and even for the janitor who mops up around the office. Writers should not have to subsidize publishers or their business experiments.

When publishers approach you about electronic rights, avoid blanket all-rights clauses that effectively give them carte blanche. Be specific. If you are licensing Web rights, identify the specific Web sites where your work may appear, otherwise it can be used

---

From the "L": Mark Kearney on "Breaking up the Fee"

When a corporate client asked author and freelancer Mark Kearney if it could print his article in the company newsletter and on the Web, here is how he responded:

The article paid $500 for about a 400-word story. One interview, very easy. I asked the guy if I could invoice him for $400 for the print version and $100 for the e-rights. He said sure, that would be fine. It doesn't mean extra money for me, but there's a record of print rights and e-rights being separate.

anywhere on the Internet. Identify which databases you agree to license. Finally, put a time limit on the licence. Consider licensing the work for the shelf life of a periodical – three months for a quarterly, for example. A one-year licence is also common.

Essentially, the two basic rules of electronic-rights licensing are: One, be specific, and two, put a time limit on it.

Moral Rights

There are three aspects to moral rights:

1. Right of Paternity: Your right to claim your work as your own.

2. Right of Integrity: If you sign away your right of integrity, other people can re-write parts of the article to suit their purposes and keep your name signed to it.

3. Right of Association: This lets you prevent others from using your work to sell something. It also prevents your work from appearing with or as a part of material that doesn't, in your opinion, fit with your reputation. For instance, if you are a photographer who works with environmental organizations, you might not want your work appear in the brochure of a multi-national oil company.

If you see a clause asking for your moral rights, beware! Moral rights have to do with the integrity of your work and your name. Often the signing over of moral rights is implicit in work-for-hire contracts. This is one very good reason not to agree to a work-for-hire arrangement. If you must sign such a contract, have the publisher spell out (and pay for) the rights it is buying. Insist on a clause that if the work is revised or adapted for another edition or medium that the publisher will offer you the opportunity to take on (and be paid) for this work.

Get it in Writing

Negotiating an agreement that is clearly understood by you and your client is key to protecting your rights. Always send a letter of intent to the client outlining all of the salient points of your agreement. This way, you can straighten out any discrepancies between your understanding and your clients' understanding before you begin. Whenever possible, use PWAC's "Standard Freelance Publication Agreement" (Appendix A).
It ensures that the points you need to clarify are fully documented. Large companies often issue purchase orders. In that case, specify the terms of agreement on the purchase order.

Always include the standard terms of copyright on your invoices and ensure that clients receive invoices before you receive payment for your work and before publication. Preferably, you

---

From the "L": Julie Barlow's Copyright Negotiation Advice — "Just Go For It!"

When a corporate communications person approached Julie Barlow about posting, on a Web site, two of her magazine profiles of wheelchair racer Chantal Petitclerc, she found out he had already used one of the articles without her permission. This is how she dealt with it:

"To his credit, he apologized for the error and agreed to pay for the right to use both stories. When the tricky issue of negotiating a fee arose, I told him I was a writer, but that my business was selling publication rights and that I considered his use of my articles 'publishing.' I asked for half my original fees for both the stories — what I would expect for a re-sale to any magazine — and asked him to check how many people had visited the site to read the article he had posted. Hardly anyone had visited the site, so we settled on a price a couple of hundred dollars lower than my original proposal, which I thought was fair. The negotiations were conducted in a courteous manner — no bullying, no bullshit. I could probably have got even more, possibly full price. I suggest if anyone is approached for use of articles on Web sites, just go for it!"

should include an invoice with your work when delivering it to the client. If a publisher responds by paying the invoice and publishing the article, and a dispute later arises, you'll be able to argue that the publication agreed to your terms or they wouldn't have published the article.

One example of the type of copyright terms that could appear on your invoice is "copyright terms: One-time Canadian print rights in English only. If the article is not published within 12 months of acceptance, all rights licensed revert to the writer without penalty or cost. All other rights reserved by author."

Copyright Tools

Tool 1: Letter of Agreement

In the absence of any other document, send a version of this letter to your editor or publisher when you receive an assignment. While it isn't as strong as a signed contract, it will act as a written record of the agreement between you. The letter is written in a format that allows for flexibility in different situations. The main body of the letter outlines a bare bones freelance writing assignment. Following it are details of the types of licences that you might negotiate and a list of optional clauses, which you might add to the letter if you feel that the situation warrants it.

Dear [editor/publisher]

Thanks for this opportunity to write for [name of publication]. I am writing to you to confirm the details of this assignment.

I will write a [length] article on [description of article]. Deadline for the article is [date]. Tentative publication of the article will be [give a date]. Payment will be [amount per word/flat fee/amount per hour] and will be made on [acceptance/publication]. This payment will be for a licence [insert licence details].

If you have any concerns about this description of the assignment, *please contact me immediately as I will be starting work right away.*

Looking forward to working with you.

Sincerely,

[writer]

Licence Details

- of one time Canadian Print rights only

- of one time North American print rights only

- of one time CD-ROM rights

- to publish on the World Wide Web site [URL], from [date] to [date]

- to publish on the World Wide Web site [URL] for [period of time]. Please inform me on what date you intend to initiate this licence.

- to publish in a commercial archival database on the World Wide Web site [URL] for one year. This licence may be renewed annually for a payment of [amount]. If I wish to revoke this licence, I must give notice one month before the licence is due to expire.

- to store on the database [name] for [period of time]. Please inform me on what date you intend to initiate this licence.

- to store on the database [name] for one year. This licence may be renewed annually for a payment of [amount]. If I wish to revoke this licence, I must give notice one month before the licence is due to expire.

Optional Clauses

Delivery and Acceptance

- I will deliver the article to you by [hard copy/computer disk/e-mail] in [insert computer program] format.

- Please notify me within 10 days of my delivery of the article whether the article is acceptable or requires revision.

If I do not hear from you in this time, I will consider that the article is accepted.

- I will be pleased to provide up to [insert number] rewrites, as required.

- Please forward a copy of any changes that you make to the article before publication.

- If the article is unacceptable and you believe that rewriting cannot make it acceptable, you will pay me a kill fee of 50 percent of the total fee. If the article is not published for any other reason, you will pay the entire fee.

Payment

- Payment will be made within [number] days of [publication/acceptance]. After this date interest of [percentage]/month will be charged.

By law, you can't charge more than two or three percent per month. Tim Perrin puts an incentive for quick payment on his invoices with the following statement: "Two percent discount for payment within 10 days of invoice date. Three percent per month interest after 30 days."

Copyright Notices

- If you do not publish the article within 12 months of delivery, all rights to the article will revert to me.

- You may store the article on your database for legal and historical reasons only.

- I retain all other rights to the article, including reprographic (photocopying), database, CD-ROM and all other electronic rights.

- If in the future you wish to use the article in any way other than is allowed by the licence agreed to in this letter, I will be pleased to negotiate terms with you at that time.

Legal

- I will alert you if there is anything in the story that could present legal risks. In the event of a libel action, I will support the magazine morally and by appearing for the defence. You will be responsible for hiring a lawyer to review the story and for paying for my defence, if necessary. If possible, you will provide a separate lawyer for me.

Tool 2: PWAC's Standard Freelance Publication Agreement

Sometimes clients or editors may ask you to write up a contract. Even if you don't use this contract, it is a very good guide to the issues that can arise in the course of a working relationship. Use it as a template or as a model to evaluate the contracts clients ask you to sign. See Appendix A for a Standard Freelance Agreement developed by PWAC. While you may not need or want to include all the items outlined in the agreement, it will help you pinpoint key areas that need discussion and inclusion in a letter of agreement.

Tool 3: Collective Power and Access Copyright

It is impossible for writers to monitor every time their work is copied and circulated. That's why a 1988 change to Canada's copyright law was so exciting. What it did was increase the ability of copyright owners, such as writers, to enforce their rights on a collective basis. Today, in Canada, we have Access Copyright (COPIBEC in Quebec), a non-profit agency established by publishers and creators that gathers together all copyright holders (writers, photographers, and illustrators, as well as book, magazine, and newspaper publishers) and works on their behalf to license public access to their articles, books, and images for a fee. From the fees it collects, Access Copyright distributes royalties back to the copyright holders. Agencies similar to Access Copyright exist for songwriters, playwrights, and filmmakers as well.

Put This Book Down!

Yes, you read it. One thing you can do immediately to protect your copyright is to put this book down and visit Access Copyright at *www.accesscopyright.ca* (or phone 1-800-893-5777). Go to the "Rightsholders" section and click on "Creator Affiliation." There you will find the Creators' Guide to Affiliation and the Creators' Affiliation Agreement. Do it right away, even if you think that your body of work won't pull in the big bucks, because you will receive money anyway. It's impossible for Access Copyright to monitor every single instance of illegal copying so it divides up the pool of royalties that can't be allocated to specific rightsholders among all of its affiliates. That means affiliates receive a cheque each year – yes, that's right, money given without asking. Sign up!

Similarly, if you write books, be sure to register them with the Public Lending Right Commission (PLRC). The PLRC does not protect copyright, but it does allocate money to writers whose books (only certain genres, however) are found in Canadian public libraries as an acknowledgement that royalties are paid only once on lending copies. See their Web site at *www.plr-dpp.ca* for more information.

Chapter 4

Savvy Writers Diversify

In the spring of 1997, *The Gazette* served Montreal freelancer Hélèna Katz with a contract demanding she sign over more rights to her work with minimal compensation. Katz decided to quit writing for the newspaper. This was a painful decision for Katz because she was earning almost half her income from *The Gazette*.

Instead of anguishing, she acted by researching new markets and sending proposal packages to a local university, several magazines, a major newspaper, a corporate newsletter, and a syndicate. By September, she says, she knew her business was back on track when she went to her mailbox and found a letter from a magazine she had pitched. "I nervously opened it and, to my relief, found they had rejected the idea. I knew I just couldn't handle one more assignment."

Tim Perrin collected this anecdote among many others when he interviewed his colleagues about how they diversified to survive. He came up with the following nine ways to cultivate new markets.

Diversify or Die!
Tim Perrin's Nine Ways to Cultivate New Markets

1. Exploit Your Specialty
In 1996, the late science writer Larry Jackson had just returned to freelancing after several years as a staff writer in the civil service. Jackson turned to the Yellow Pages to look for companies that could benefit from his expertise as a science writer. "Most scientists and engineers can't write and a lot of them know it.

Many hate it but can't avoid it, because their business runs on proposals, grant applications, and reports. The more competitive it gets, the more they need incisive prose." Jackson found some likely companies and approached them until he had a greater diversity of clients.

2. Expand Your Horizons
If you live in a smaller centre – or even a big city – don't be afraid to look to nearby cities or even nation-wide for clients. Use your local library's collection of telephone books or search the World Wide Web. Clients don't need to see you that often, if at all; it's the work that matters.

3. Advertise
If you are strategic, advertising can really pay off. I (Tim) placed a small ad in *InfoWeek* offering to write computer documentation. That $150 investment turned into a long-term relationship with a California publishing company worth more than $35,000 over three years writing manuals for companies from Japan, California, Washington, and New Jersey.

4. Build Relationships
Barbara Florio Graham makes relationship-building a year round activity. Once she has targeted potential clients, she makes an initial contact, then works to build trust and familiarity. She recommends watching the business pages for anything that mentions companies you are trying to recruit as clients. She copies information that is of interest to her prospects onto a sheet of her letterhead, writes a short personal note, and passes it along to her contact. "It catches attention," she says.

5. Stretch Your Skills
Montreal freelancer Heather Pengelley was doing regular assignments for a consumer magazine, a city magazine, and a lifestyle magazine. She was also doing the odd assignment for a small medical publisher who was, in her words, "printing my articles without verbs that I know were there in the first place."

Pengelley decided to "fire" that client and dropped by the office to tell the publisher. He admitted he was overworked, had been using his secretary for copy editing and asked her if she would be interested in freelance editing the publication for which she had been writing. It was a stretch but Pengelley took the job on.

Within six months, all three of her other major markets disappeared off the supermarket shelves. Pengelley's stretch into the medical field turned out to be her lifesaver. She now does much of her work in that sector which she says has been "recession proof." "Demands within this market have shifted every few years from publications to videos to slide presentations," she says. "I have diversified my skills again and again and again."

6. Cross Genre Boundaries

James Joseph, a Los Angeles-based member of the American Society of Journalists and Authors, says that for highly diversified writers, there need never be tough times. He should know. He has been a successful freelancer for more than 40 years. Joseph uses work in one genre to spark sales in others. When he finished one screenplay, he had the accompanying book proposal out to publishers. "This month, I will pitch to prospective motion picture and TV series producers no fewer than six screen/TV concepts, all of them based on my book and article research," he says.

7. Develop an Eye for Spin-Off Story Ideas

Joseph also has a keen eye for story possibilities that others have missed. He read a third-person story in one magazine and realized it would make a great first-person tale. He contacted the person involved and spun the first-person story into magazine, television, and movie sales. "That's diversification," he says. "Magazine article + TV script + screenplay = big bucks!"

8. Synergize Your Skills into Sidelines

Toronto freelancer Denyse O'Leary has written a book, *Editing as a Sideline* (available through PWAC), geared toward helping writers develop and use their editing skills to help support their writing projects. She encourages writers to diversify in ways that have synergy such as editing, graphic arts, translation, teaching, et cetera.

"By synergy, I mean the two businesses feed each other clients naturally. I discourage diversification where synergy is unlikely – editing and running a day care centre, for example," she says.

9. Keep Your Work Out There

Perhaps the best piece of advice I ever received on multiplying my markets came from veteran writer Arturo F. "Arky" Gonzalez:

First, "Write and mail a query a day." It's a challenging pace but it pays off. Second, "Never sleep with your ideas." If a query comes back rejected, send it back out to a new market *the same day*. In a month, you'll have two-dozen ideas out there. In two months, it will be four dozen, in three months, six. You only have to sell a few of them to stay profitably busy.

The Internal Exam

If you are having problems getting started, it's time for some internal research. The prerequisite to any marketing effort is to know two basic things: One, the expertise that you offer, and two, to whom you want to offer it. If you haven't created a plan for yourself or your business yet, refer to Chapter One. After you've done that, here is a series of questions, put together by Paul Lima to help you create a marketing strategy:

- Who are you?
- What is your background: education, employment, and significant life experiences?
- What are your hobbies and interests?
- What are you passionate about?
- What do you know?
- What don't you know but would like to find out about?
- What would you love to write about?
- What would you like to write about?

- What can you write about?
- Why?
- Why you?

With your answers, immerse yourself in the stacks at the library, the phone book, on the Web, et cetera. Look for people, organizations, and publications that you should get to know and who might need what you have to offer.

If you'd like some additional inspiration, the classic *What Color is Your Parachute?* by Richard Nelson Bolles includes a section on how to start your own business. The book has a companion site at www.jobhuntersbible.com.

Newspapers and Magazines: Some Words on the Query Letter

The key to breaking into magazines is to write an *outstanding* query letter. In a query, writers are essentially writing an editor to tell them a story. Often the first paragraph of the query ends up as the lead of the article. Newspapers and the sections within those newspapers vary on queries. Some want to see finished articles on spec. Others prefer short one-to-five paragraph queries.

There are as many different approaches and formats (e-mail, fax, snail mail) to the query letter as there are editors. The best thing is to do some detective work on the particular editor that you are planning to pitch. Ask around for other writers who have had contact with the editor to find his or her preferences, or, failing that, have a friendly chat with the assistant who answers the phone at the publication. (Beware! Have your ideas ready because you never know when the editor will pick up the phone!)

Bonnie Reichert, former editor of *Today's Parent* and now a freelance writer, says good queries are useful not only for the editor, but also for the writer. "A good query pops out in a pile of mail, so give it all you've got, sketch out a story. From a writer's point of view, the query will not only get work, but will also help later as you write. Look at the query as a chance to write your own assignment letter."

Reichart says the harder it is for you to describe the story to a friend, the more you need to tighten the idea. "It should be tight, snappy, give a bit of the tone and flavour of the story, and show you know the magazine, so be sure that before you pitch, look at the publication's back issues. Go back six months to ensure the idea hasn't been done."

For a more in-depth look at queries, PWAC has resources at *www.pwactoronto.org*. Go to "Notes from Evening Seminars" and look at the notes from PWAC Toronto's Query Lab and "Finding New Markets and Recycling Articles."

Radio: Sound Rules the Day

A top-notch query is also the key to breaking into radio. What makes radio queries different is that you have to keep in mind that sound and vivid descriptions are the keys to telling your story.

Iris Yudai, a radio producer for the CBC, advises freelancers to tell the producer about the sound you will include in your piece. Radio producers are also keen for stories in which "something will happen on the air." They want you to take the listener on a journey with your sound, interviews, and storytelling.

For more discussion on pitching to radio, visit *www.pwactoronto.org*. Go to "Notes from Evening Seminars" and look at "Look Who's Talking: Freelancing for Radio." At *www.cbc.ca/outfront* CBC producers have created a Radio Resource Centre for beginners. The CBC's *Outfront* program is an excellent show to get your feet wet because it's geared toward working with people who have little radio experience.

Television: Contacts are the Key

Writers most commonly get their start as researchers for television or documentary film. PWACer Alex Roslin, a Montreal writer and researcher for CBC-TV's investigative magazine show *Disclosure*, got his TV break through his print magazine work. One of his sources hooked him up with a journalist from another CBC investigative show, *The Fifth Estate*, who was looking for a researcher. That contact led to another contact at *Disclosure*, another CBC production.

"If you are doing an investigative story for a magazine, shows such as *The Fifth Estate*, *Disclosure*, or *Marketplace* often pay for ideas or hire freelancers to develop stories," he says. "Or, if you are a food writer, pitch to the cooking shows, if you are a travel writer, pitch to the travel shows et cetera." Roslin says it is key to remember that television stories are a big commitment and take many resources to create. So, your pitch has to be that much more convincing to get a producer to invest the money and time. Of course, it helps if you know someone who knows someone, so work your network for information and connections.

If you want to break into television or film drama, Canadian author and creative writing professor W.D. Valgardson advises that you hit the pavement to find a director who likes your work. "There is so little consistent work in Canadian radio and television drama, or for original stage plays that the production of a writer's work is often dependent on the working relationship between a writer and director," he says. Valgardson strongly advocates to his students that they hang on to the dramatic rights to their work and learn to adapt their stories to the airwaves or stage. "The reason for learning to adapt material from one form to another is simple – money. You get peanuts for the rights to a short story. But the last short story of mine that I adapted for TV paid $14,000. If someone else did the adaptation, they'd have the $14,000 and I'd have a couple of hundred dollars," he says. "I tell my students, 'I'm a writer. I can write anything.' The technique of each genre is easily learnable. Learn it. Get the work. Get the money. Money matters. And it matters more in your pocket than in someone else's."

The Corporate Sector

For writers who balk at the thought of lending their journalism skills and writing talent to corporate ends, remember that media companies are among the biggest corporations in existence today. The choice about where you want to market your skills is a personal one. Freelancers who take this route generally find that clients in corporate sectors other than the media value journalism skills highly. If you decide to take on some corporate clients to help fund your journalism projects, it is important to be clear with both your clients and your editors about where your interests lie to avoid conflicts of interest.

What You Bring to the Corporate Market

Corporate employers like working with freelance writers for a number of reasons. You bring incredible value to a company because:

- They can hire you on a per project basis.
- You supply your own office space and equipment.
- They don't pay your benefits or take responsibility for your job security.
- Most business people either can't, or don't have the time to write so you are taking care of what they perceive as a very big headache.
- With a background in journalism, you bring assertiveness and research skills that many corporate employees lack.
- As an outsider, you can avoid the day-to-day internal politics.
- As an outsider, you can provide an objective opinion about the company's message and literature.
- You bring a diversity of experiences to the job.
- Companies place a high value on people who have been writers or broadcasters for major media outlets.

If You Want to Break In

Although it helps in any sector to "look professional" when making that first appearance, it is particularly critical with corporate clients. Trade your writing skills with a graphic designer for a spiffy business card, letterhead, and Web site interface. Put together a marketing portfolio to highlight your unique skills, experiences, and past projects. Understand that when you enter the office of a corporate client you are a consultant who is in the business of providing solutions. While clients may be fascinated about your upcoming novel on a personal level, from a business perspective they want to know you are the answer to the particular problem they are facing – how to get that report, press release, Web site copy, brochure, et cetera, researched and written by deadline. It is up to you to demonstrate your ability, and then deliver. Winning new corporate clients is most often as simple as that.

Manage the Process and the People

Often you know more about the process that goes into producing a newsletter, press release, brochure, et cetera, than your client does. Regardless, it is critical when you take on a corporate client that you make the process clear and draw attention to potential problem areas before the project begins. Put the process in writing, have it approved, and keep a paper trail.

John Mason, director of marketing and communications for Career Edge, a national internship program, advises that as clients give their approval to the various steps in the process, have them sign an "approvals sheet" that you provide. (A simple chart with names, signatures, and dates will do). This way, you avoid taking the heat for any wrong decisions they make.

Corporate clients are interested in the bottom line and will demand quotes early on in the process. To negotiate this discussion, see Paul Lima's Estimating Checklist on page 31. Don't offer below-standard rates. Corporate clients often question the professionalism of consultants who price too low – and so they should. Go for top rates and give top-rate work.

Also, if you want to break into the corporate market, be sure to sign up for a GST number. Not having a GST number suggests that you either make less than $30,000 per year or you are not keeping your books properly. This causes concern for an employer whose job may depend on your ability to deliver quality work on time.

The Money Myth About Non-Profits

Many people assume that just because non-profits are not in the business of making money they don't have any. Not true. Even non-profits that aren't rich often find project money. Freelancers are perfect for this work because of their ability to come and go from project to project. Marketing to the non-profit sector is similar to marketing to for-profit companies — it's a combination of networking and building a reputation in your specialty area. And people will pay top rates if they see it is a cost-effective decision for them to do so.

Heather Kent writes for a quarterly non-profit newsletter that gets revenue from advertising and sponsorships. She negotiated $75 per hour by telling her client that she can achieve a lot in an hour. She has developed a good working relationship over the last year because she gives the client a very clear idea, with each issue, just what she will produce in the 20 hours for which she generally contracts. "Before I came along, they would delay the newsletter as long as possible, then go out and get experts to contribute for free, then try and edit it themselves," says Kent. "Not only do I save them a lot of time, but they like the new style and they tell me they have received great feedback. So they feel they are getting value for their money. And they are!"

Even if a non-profit doesn't have a budget to pay you a decent rate, you can often negotiate for a tax receipt, an advertisement, or other practical things to help your business. Writer Gil Parker bartered his press-release writing skills in exchange for free entry to a conference on Adventure Therapy — which would have cost him $450. He also negotiated rights to interview some of the top speakers. Even before attending the conference, he had two articles already commissioned by publications. By the end of the conference, he had three more story ideas he planned to query.

A great source for non-profit information and work opportunities is *www.charityvillage.ca*.

Government: Teamwork, Contacts, Persistence, and Dumb Luck

Marketing to the government is like marketing to hundreds of different (and often competing) companies. The three levels, federal, provincial, and municipal, have different departments and each department has its own corporate culture.

Governments are starting to put their tenders online using databases, such as *www.merx.com*, which includes the federal government and the 10 provincial governments. British Columbia also has its own database at *www.bcbid.gov.ca*. Each day there are about a hundred postings on MERX. Freelancer Deborah Schoen says that the contracts are worth over $25,000 and she usually sees opportunities for writers about twice each month. The tenders are usually standing offers where departments are looking for writers to be available for regular work on pretty much an on-call basis. Some last for one year, others last for three months.

Writer Dale Kerr cautions that there is no guarantee of work once a writer gets a standing offer. "I have had a standing offer with one government department for $100,000 per year (this is an upper limit for the amount of work) for the past four years and have yet to earn a cent from it," she says. When the work does flow, these contracts tend to be a lot for one person. Schoen has had at least one other researcher/writer as well as expert advisors work with her on all of her MERX contracts.

In the last couple of years, the MERX subscription rate has increased dramatically – from about $7 per month to $35 per month. Kerr, who was subscribed through her husband's engineering company, quit the subscription after the fee hike because it stopped being worthwhile. She recommends that instead of subscribing, writers check the database regularly and pay the non-subscriber rate to get the detailed request for proposal once they see something they would really like to bid on.

An important factor to consider when going the MERX-route is that proposals are a lot of work. Kerr says she has done proposals that have taken over a week of solid work to write. Instead, Kerr says she gets most of her work because she knows the people involved. Her most successful marketing strategy is to attend conferences and seminars to meet the technical people involved with government projects. She says she can negotiate much better rates by dealing directly with the technical people. When Schoen took a contract to cover a public health symposium, it wasn't big money, but it was a potent marketing opportunity. The work gave her a chance to meet each of the presenters – 20 new contacts in her field.

Writing a Proposal for Government Work

According to Dale Kerr, the most important thing to remember about a proposal is that it has to sell itself. The key aspects are the project and needs summaries. Don't simply regurgitate the RFP (request for proposal entries commonly found on MERX) but add something original to indicate you have thought about the work and why it is important. Once you've convinced them you understand their needs, provide a detailed methodology. "I will typically break a project down into steps and be specific about, for instance, the number of references I will seek and say, for example, 'I will interview between five and 10 people,'" says Kerr. "Always use a range as you may not be able to find 10 people who are appropriate for the project and then you'll be stuck. I also try to list the resources I will use, again giving myself a bit of leeway by saying, 'I will consult up to 10 publications including... and list at least three.'"

Hélèna Katz stumbled across a prospect while surfing the Web. She found a newsletter put out by a federal ministry and subscribed. When she started reading it, she noticed by-lines on the pieces, so she phoned up the ministry to ask if they used freelancers. The answer was "Yes." After Katz sent off a package and followed up, the newsletter editors said they were very interested. Two months went by so Katz contacted them again to tell them about an upcoming trip to Ottawa and they agreed to a meeting. The meeting went well, but two more months passed before they finally called. "We sometimes think that if a marketing pitch doesn't work right away then it isn't going to work at all. But really, you have to put out a whole lot of feelers to a whole lot of people. Some will pan out right away and some may take months, even years."

Kerr then includes a work flow chart to indicate the length of time for each step. "Be very specific about the deliverables. Typically the government wants on-going updates which can be as simple as a letter report or as detailed as the complete draft of a chapter." Kerr says she often ties payments to deliverables. For example, after completing interviews she will prepare a letter summarizing who has been interviewed and invoice for ten percent of the full contract value.

One warning: Don't tie payments to milestones that are too big. Kerr says she once made the mistake of tying a 50 percent payment to the completion of a first draft on a large project. It took over a year.

Finally, if contracts are small enough, government departments don't have to go through a competitive tendering process. Kerr says if you get wind of some work that needs doing, keep your fee below this threshold, and you can often get the work with only a short letter proposal.

Chapter 5

Savvy Writers Recycle

Toss, Flip, and Turn:
Recycling and the Successful Freelancer

Talk to writers who recycle their work and the message is simple: You can't afford not to do it. Hélèna Katz puts it succinctly: "I read an article a long time ago where a guy was saying people are too busy to recycle their work. That's like saying 'I'm too busy running off to my job at McDonald's to pick up that $500 bill on the sidewalk.'"

Indeed, Barbara Florio Graham says a common problem among writers is that they spend too much time writing and not enough time recycling their work. To pay the bills as a writer, make the most money you can out of every project. What works for the environment, works for the writer.

Here are some recycling techniques from PWAC's best prose conservationists:

1. The straight re-sell:
As long as it's a non-competing publication, it's fair game to sell the same piece more than once. When Paul Lima types the keywords "Barry Lewis" into his computer, five entries come up with the lead "Barry Lewis has a dog-eared passport..." Over three years, he has sold this article five times.

2. Stretch or shrink:
Turn a larger piece into a sidebar or "front of the book piece," or expand a side bar into a bigger piece. Katz took a piece she did for the (now defunct) *Canadian Airlines* magazine and turned it into a point-form side bar for *Canadian Living*.

3. Change the slant:

Find as many different angles to the story as you can during the research phase. While interviewing the executive director of the Trans Canada Trail about his marketing strategy, Katz asked him which school he graduated from. She sold a profile to his alumni magazine. She also added questions about the trail construction and sold that story to a news service. She then did a straight news piece on the trail for an American outdoor magazine that involved a re-interview with the executive director, but she was able to re-use her background research.

4. Change the tone or point of view:

Turn a serious piece to satire or make a piece of reportage into a first-person essay.

5. Local to national to international:

Add one or two interviews to make a local piece national, international, or vice versa. Katz did a piece on hemp marketing

Waste Not, Want Not

A conservationist approach also applies to many other areas of your business. Barbara Florio Graham offers up some tips:

• **Never waste a stamp:** Florio Graham includes bookmarks or brochures for her books with practically every item she sends in the mail.

• **Never waste a pitch:** When you are querying, think strategically about the clips you send. A little phrase such as "Enclosed are some of my previously published articles. I've included a short piece on 'How to Teach your Dog to Communicate'

which may work for your 'Tips for Trainers' section...."

• **Re-use your contacts:** Everybody has a network, whether professional or informal. Florio Graham diligently enters everybody she meets into a database with notes about their interests, where they live, et cetera. To publicize her book *Musings/Mewsings*, she looked through her contacts and targeted people across Canada and the US who she thought might circulate promotional bookmarks in exchange for a complimentary copy.

for Canada's *Marketing Magazine*, then found a couple of US sources to re-work it for an American news service.

6. Translate (or hire a translator):

When Katz was approached by a French publication to re-print her article about disabled skiers, published in *Abilities* magazine, she got more for the French version than she did for the original English version. She did a rough translation and then hired a friend to polish it up and still made $275.

7. Slice and dice:

Barbara Florio Graham says "Stop," if you are struggling to squeeze fascinating material into a piece. Chances are you have another piece or maybe your fragments stand up on their own as small filler pieces or tips-based sidebars. Also take a look at your articles and pieces of articles to see if you can combine them for new angles or "round-up" pieces.

The key to recycling is to think about it from the outset. During your research, keep your eyes open for different angles, markets, and work the relevant questions into your interviews. Also keep your eyes and ears open for the quirky alleyways in your piece that can lead to new pieces. Be patient with yourself. As Katz says, recycling is like riding a bicycle. The whole charade seems slow and tedious at first, but as you learn the right balance of spotting new story ideas, finding the right market, and negotiating with confidence, you get into a "groove."

For those writers who are tired of a story once they've cranked out that full-length feature, Katz recommends setting the research aside for now and then recycling it a bit later. She has a cabinet drawer of story files that she browses regularly for recycling possibilities. Florio Graham is more systematic. She keeps a sheet for each article where she lists the topic, article title, date created, word count, date it was first sold, rights licensed, and payment. Then she lists the other types of articles she thinks she could create from the research and potential markets.

The *Canadian Writer's Market* and *Writer's Market* from the US are two important market research tools to keep handy. And, most writers regularly take time to flip through and analyze new magazines. At the time of writing, PWAC is in the process of creating a Canadian magazine and newspaper database for members to pool their markets knowledge and experiences.

Rights and the Recycling Writer

Writers who recycle have to read and understand their contracts. Get to know contract clauses to empower yourself during negotiation. For more on this, see Chapter Three.

Chapter 6

Savvy Writers Can Make Six Figures

Ann Douglas has become a one-woman writing industry after publishing 21 books in five years. She has established herself as a parenting expert while having fun with projects, such as a book on body image co-written with her daughter and a history of great Canadian women. At a 2001 PWAC conference, she shared her ideas about what it takes to make six figures as a writer.

Ann Douglas' Tips for Writing Nirvana

1. Understanding what it takes:
The first step to making a decent income is to set some clear financial objectives. Decide how much you want to make each year and how many projects you will have to complete each month and each week in order to generate that kind of income. You will likely find this number-crunching exercise encourages you to take a long, hard look at your rates. After all, you're pretty much sentencing yourself to working around the clock if the bulk of your markets are concentrated at the low end of the writing food chain.

2. Think long-term:
Ask yourself where the publishing industry is headed and where you hope to be in five to 10 years time. What kinds of work do you want to be doing? How much money do you want to be making? What do you need to be doing today to ensure that you ultimately meet those goals?

3. Bridges and stepping stones:
If you don't have the credentials, experience, or contacts to be doing the writing work you want to be doing, look for stepping-

stones to take you there. Write a series book to establish yourself as an author. Pitch a bunch of short, service-oriented "front of the book" pieces for the magazine of your dreams and hope they will eventually trust you with a feature. And let your editors know what you want. I landed my very favourite writing gig – a pregnancy humour column for *Flare Pregnancy* – by mentioning to my editor that I'd love to write something along those lines. You may not always get what you want, but you definitely won't get it if you don't ask.

4. Evaluate your return on investment:
Consider the income you generate during any given time period. Rather than wasting a couple of hours writing up a pitch for a 200-word story that may pay at most a couple of hundred bucks, use that same amount of effort to come up with a highly saleable idea for a book project – or better yet an entire book series. Sometimes it's better to turn down poorer paying work in order to buy yourself time to market more effectively and land better-paying work.

5. Don't put all your eggs in one publishing basket:
Ours is a highly volatile industry that is hit with its fair share of ups and downs. (Yes, Virginia, there are ups. You just have to be watching carefully to spot them!) If you are diversified (or to use the current lingo, if you have "multiple streams of income"), you won't be hit quite so hard by a downturn in the magazine or book publishing sector.

6. Write a book:
Writing for magazines and newspapers is a bit like living from paycheque to paycheque. There's no built-in royalty stream. Books are different (if you sign a decent book contract): They can provide for a steady stream of income for the entire time your book is in print. So if you're sick of living hand to mouth, you might want to think about writing a couple of books. Not only will the book provide you with added income by way of

royalties, it'll boost your credibility as a writer and allow you to land more plum writing assignments.

7. Hedge your bets:

If you're counting on a bestseller to finance your retirement, I hate to have to be the one to break it to you, but here goes: You have a better chance of getting hit by lightning than of making it to the number one spot on *The New York Times* bestseller list, and only slightly better odds of making it to the top of *The Globe and Mail* bestseller list. (10 Canadians get hit by lightning each year and there are, at most, 52 cracks at the number one spot on *The Globe and Mail* bestseller list annually.) Does this mean that you're doomed to retire broke? Not at all! If you can't crack the number one spot, simply set your sights on having a lot of top-selling, mid-list titles. After all, having five books that sell 20,000 copies each can earn you every bit as much as having a single title that sells 100,000 copies.

8. Make hay while the sun shines:

Murphy's Law of Freelancing goes something like this: If a particular freelance gig seems too good to be true, it probably is, so cash in quickly. I had the good fortune to make a lot of money when some of the leading US Web sites were throwing $2 US a word at freelancers and asking them to write pages and pages of copy overnight. I once managed to make $5400 in a single evening – $1700 an hour for my time! I knew it was too good to last, so I took the work while it was there, invoiced promptly, cashed my cheques more promptly still, and then started looking for more solvent pastures when the dot com bubble began to burst.

9. Be both a specialist and a generalist:

You can make a lot of money as a specialist because you can recycle research and interviews; cross-promote books and speaking engagements in the bio line that often accompanies your articles; and so on. But it can be dangerous to have all your eggs in one basket. I specialize in writing about pregnancy and babies so I'm starting to develop some new specialties that will hopefully help to pay my bills once my "baby days" are behind me: Women's health, women's pop culture, and writing about writing.

10. Play favourites:
Give the royal treatments to your "A clients" – the ones who treat you well and pay you even better. Fit the "B clients" on your to-do list only when time permits. And remember, it's never worth working for a jerk.

11. Don't sign contracts you will regret:
Magazine, newspaper, and Web site contracts that wrestle away all rights or book contracts that pay you as a contractor and deny you a slice of the royalty pie make it difficult to earn a living. So unless they're paying you the king's ransom up-front, it probably doesn't make business sense.

12. Be passionate about what you do:
Only take on projects that you're willing to put heart and soul into. Otherwise you're short-changing your editor and yourself. Besides when you write about things that really matter to you, you'll hardly feel like you're working at all. We writers are fortunate to be in a line of work that allows us to truly make a difference in this world – to help people, to change lives. And at the end of the day that is worth more than any paycheque, six figures or not. It's the ultimate dividend.

The Last Word
So… all it takes to make a living as a writer is a little strategy mixed with heaps of creativity and hard work. Oh… and a lot of patience.

Every freelancer quoted in this book knows that it is one thing to talk about being brave and sticking up for your rights and proper pay but another thing altogether to do it. Along the way there will be mistakes, defeats, and those days when you just push your chair away from the desk and go for a long, long walk – or worse, pull the covers over your head in the morning and pray it will all go away. When it happens, remember that you are not alone. We learn not only from seeking advice but also from our mistakes. And the best mistakes (and successes!) come from those moments when we were brave enough to try.

It's time to bust that myth that real writers live in poverty. Step forward with confidence in your own talent and professionalism and seek out some fellow savvy freelancers whom you can trust and who inspire you. The irony is that only by working together will we keep that delicious freedom inherent in the freelance way of life.

Appendix A

Periodical Writers Association of Canada
(Note: This document may be downloaded at www.writers.ca)

Standard Freelance Publication Agreement

This agreement is between

_____

(the "Writer")

And

_____

(the "Publisher/Client")

DESCRIPTION OF ASSIGNMENT:

_____

WORKING TITLE:

_____

BY-LINE TO READ:

_____

APPROXIMATE LENGTH OF ARTICLE:

_____

DEADLINE:

_____

TENTATIVE PUBLICATION DATE: TO BE PUBLISHED NO LATER THAN:
____/____/____   ____/____/____

NAME OF PUBLICATION:

_____

EDITOR OR OTHER REPRESENTATIVE OF PUBLISHER/CLIENT:

_____

(the "Editor")

PRINT RIGHTS LICENSED (check):
☐ One-time Canadian Print Rights
☐ One-time North American Print Rights
☐ English (original language)
☐ French (original language)
FEE FOR PRINT RIGHTS LICENSED: $ _____

☐ One-time Canadian Print Rights in translation
☐ One-time North American Print Rights in translation
FEE FOR ONE-TIME USE IN TRANSLATION: $ _____

73

WEB SITE RIGHTS LICENSED:
Yes ☐   No ☐
If yes, complete the following details:

Name of Web site:

_____

URL:

_____

Such right is (check one): exclusive ☐ non-exclusive ☐
And is granted for a period of (check one):
☐ 24-hr day of publication   ☐ 7 days   ☐ 15 days   ☐ 30 days
☐ 3 months   ☐ 6 months   ☐ 1 year
This license may be renewed annually for payment of $ _____
If the writer wishes to revoke this license, the writer must give notice one
month before the license is due to expire.
FEE FOR WEB SITE RIGHTS LICENSED: $ _____

COMMERCIAL ARCHIVAL DATABASES:
User-Fee Database Rights Licensed: Yes ☐   No ☐
Right to publish in a commercial archival database on the World Wide Web site:
_____ (URL) for one year. This license
may be renewed annually for payment of $_____
If the writer wishes to revoke this license, the writer must give notice one
month before the license is due to expire.
FEE FOR DATABASE RIGHTS LICENSED: $_____
(plus 50% of gross proceeds received by or on behalf
of the Publisher for each re-publication)

One-time CD-ROM Rights Licensed: Yes ☐   No ☐
Right to include in a CD-ROM _____ (name)
for _____ (period of time) commencing
on _____ (date)
FEE FOR CD-ROM RIGHTS LICENSED: $_____

GENERAL EXPENSES:
The Publisher/Client agrees to reimburse the Writer for direct expenses incurred
in fulfilling this agreement. Such expenses shall include photocopying, fax,
long-distance telephone calls, Internet charges, couriers, and

_____

_____

Such expenses will not exceed a maximum amount of $_____
except with the Publisher/Client's agreement.

TRAVEL EXPENSES:
The Publication agrees to reimburse the Writer for travel expenses to a
maximum amount of $_____ except with the Publisher/Client's
agreement. Travel expenses will include:

_____

The Writer agrees to write, and the Publisher/Client agrees to publish, a manuscript in accordance with the following Terms of Agreement. This agreement includes the above specifications and any attached materials initialed by both parties. The fee specified in this agreement does not include Goods and Services (GST) or other applicable national or provincial sales taxes.

Terms of Agreement

PART I: THE WRITER'S OBLIGATIONS

1. TRUTHFULNESS AND ACCURACY

1.1 The Writer will not deliberately write a dishonest, plagiarized, or inaccurate statement into the manuscript. The Writer shall reveal any conflict of interest or possible conflict of interest to a representative of the Publisher/Client, hereinafter called Editor, upon receiving the assignment.

2. SOURCES

2.1 The Writer will be prepared to support all statements in the manuscript and to assist the checker in verifying statements of fact.

2.2 In stories involving trials, public hearings or other controversial subject matter, the Writer will try to check all sources against a transcript of the proceedings, if one is available.

3. LIBEL

3.1 The Writer shall alert the Editor to special circumstances regarding a story that could present legal risks to the Publisher/Client. In the case of a libel action, the Writer shall support the Publisher/Client morally and by appearing for the defence, if requested.

4. DEADLINES

4.1 The Writer shall deliver a clean, typed, or word-processed manuscript on or before the agreed deadline. If the Writer cannot meet the deadline, the Writer shall give the Editor reasonable notice in advance of the agreed deadline. The Writer may not set a new deadline without the Editor's consent.

4.2 If the Writer fails to complete the assignment on deadline without the Editor's consent to an extension, the Editor has the right to terminate this agreement and make no further payment to the Writer.

5. REVISIONS

5.1 The Writer and Editor will discuss the content, style, revisions, focus, and point of view to be used in the manuscript. The Writer will then use his or her best efforts to write the article within the agreed parameters and will obtain the consent of the Editor before departing from any of them.

5.2 If the manuscript, as submitted, fails to fall within the agreed parameters, the Editor may require the Writer to revise the manuscript. The Writer and Editor will agree on the suitable time for making these revisions and any minor updates.

6. UPDATING

6.1 If delays in publication or changes in the circumstances surrounding a subject make extensive updating of a manuscript necessary, the Writer will update the manuscript, for a fee to be negotiated, if his or her other commitments permit.

6.2 If unable to update the manuscript, the Writer may either authorize the publication to update the manuscript, subject to Section 12, or may revert his or her rights to the manuscript.

7. EDITORIAL CHANGES

7.1 The Writer will be available for discussion and consultation during the editing process.

7.2 The Writer will notify the Editor in writing if, after reading the final edited version of the manuscript, he or she wishes to withdraw his or her name from the manuscript before its publication.

8. EXPENSES

8.1 The Writer will not incur any extraordinary expenses without prior consent of the Editor.

8.2 Within 60 days of acceptance of the final manuscript, the Writer shall claim reimbursement for expenses and/or account for any amount received for expenses in advance, and the Publisher/Client shall make such reimbursement within 10 days of the receipt of the Writer's account of expenses.

PART II: THE PUBLICATION'S OBLIGATIONS
9. SOURCES

9.1 The Publisher/Client will respect any promises of confidentiality the Writer has made in the course of obtaining information.

10. LIBEL

10.1 Where advisable, the Publisher/Client will hire a lawyer to review the manuscript for libel implications.

10.2 In the case of a libel action, the Publisher/Client will morally support the Writer. If the Writer requests it, the Publisher/Client will pay the costs of the Writer's defence. Where appropriate, the Publisher/Client will provide the Writer with a separate lawyer.

11. REVISIONS

11.1 In requesting revisions to a manuscript, the Editor will give reasonable, detailed instructions as to the nature and extent of the required changes.

11.2 If the Editor requests revisions that involve significant departure from the previously agreed upon approach or treatment, the Writer may refuse to revise the manuscript and still be entitled to full payment. If the Writer agrees to do the revisions, he or she will be paid for the time spent rewriting at a rate or for a fee to be negotiated.

11.3 "Significant departures" include: (a) new research; (b) change of focus; (c) change of style; (d) change of opinion or point of view.

12. UPDATING

12.1 If the manuscript requires extensive updating for the reasons mentioned in Section 6, the Editor will offer the Writer first opportunity to do the updating.

12.2 The Publisher/Client will pay the Writer for updating at a rate to be negotiated.

12.3 If a person other than the Writer does the updating, the Editor will give the Writer an opportunity to review the changes and to remove his or her name from the published article in accordance with Section 13.

13. EDITORIAL CHANGES

13.1 The Editor shall inform the Writer of changes in the edited version of the manuscript while there is still time to discuss and reach an agreement on such changes.

13.2 The Editor will give the Writer an opportunity to read the final edited version of the manuscript reasonably in advance of its publication.

13.3 The Publisher/Client must withdraw the Writer's name for use in connection with the published article, if the Writer so notifies the Editor in writing.

14. ACCEPTANCE AND PAYMENT

14.1 The Editor will notify the Writer of his or her acceptance or rejection of the manuscript within 15 days of (a) delivery of the manuscript, or (b) the deadline, whichever is later; otherwise the manuscript shall be considered accepted by the Publisher/Client.

14.2 The Publisher/Client will pay the agreed fee to the Writer within 10 days of acceptance of the manuscript and will pay expenses in full within 10 days of receiving the Writer's account of expenses.

14.3 If for any reasons unrelated to the originally agreed upon requirements of the assignment, the Publisher/Client decides not to use the delivered manuscript, the Publisher/Client will pay the Writer the agreed fee and expenses in full.

14.4 If the manuscript is accepted by the Editor or another person with apparent authority to do so and is later considered to be unacceptable, the Publisher/Client will pay the Writer the agreed fee and expenses in full.

15. KILL FEE

15.1 If the Writer delivers a manuscript that fails to meet the originally agreed upon requirements of the assignment and if the Editor considers that the manuscript cannot be made acceptable through rewriting, the Editor may terminate the assignment by providing the Writer with written notice and paying the Writer not less than one half of the agreed fee, plus the Writer's expenses to date.

15.2 If, in the course of research or during the writing of a manuscript, the Writer concludes that the information available will not result in a satisfactory article, the Writer will inform the Editor and give reasons to discontinue the assignment. If the Editor agrees, the assignment is terminated. The Publisher/Client will pay a reasonable fee, to be negotiated, to compensate the Writer for work done prior to termination, on presentation of the Writer's research documentation.

15.3 If the Editor wishes to cancel this agreement after work has begun, the Publication will pay a reasonable fee, to be negotiated, to compensate the Writer for work done prior to termination.

16. EXPENSES

16.1 If no limitation is specified in writing, the Publication will reimburse the Writer for all customary and normal out-of-pocket expenses incurred in completing this assignment.

PART III: RIGHTS
17. COPYRIGHT

17.1 The Writer retains the copyright in all manuscripts written under this agreement, whether or not an article is published.

17.2 Unless the parties agree otherwise in writing, this agreement licenses to the Publisher/Client only those rights indicated on the first page of this agreement. Unless specified otherwise, the Publisher/Client has the right to enter the manuscript into and retrieve the manuscript from a computerized information storage and retrieval system only for the purpose of preparing the manuscript for publication, and may store the article in its database for legal purposes only, including documentation of the assignment.

17.3 No license, including Web site rights, granted under this agreement, is valid until the Writer has received all of the agreed upon fee.

17.4 All rights not specifically licensed to the Publisher/Client remain the Writer's exclusively. These rights may include reprint rights, electronic rights, photocopying and other reprography rights, and the right to enter the manuscript into or retrieve it from a computerized information storage and retrieval system for purposes other than publication under the terms of this agreement.

17.5 Where a manuscript is rejected, and in all other instances where the assignment is terminated prior to publication of the article, all rights revert to the Writer, who may submit the manuscript elsewhere for publication.

18. REVERSION OF RIGHTS

18.1 If the Publisher/Client accepts a manuscript but does not publish it within 12 months of acceptance, the Writer shall have the option to revert, by written notice, all rights licensed herein without penalty or cost.

18.2 If under this agreement the Publisher/Client acquires a license for the Web site rights to a work previously or simultaneously published in either print or electronic format, either by the Publisher/Client or a third party, and does not publish it on its Web site within 6 months of the signing of this agreement, the Writer shall have the option to revert such rights without penalty.

18.3 If the assignment terminates prior to publication, all rights granted under this agreement shall revert to the Writer. The Publisher/Client may not publish the manuscript but may retain a copy only for the purposes of documenting the assignment.

PART IV: MEDIATION AND ARBITRATION
19. MEDIATION
19.1 When the Writer and Publisher/Client disagree over the interpretation of this agreement, they may each appoint one representative who will endeavour to settle the dispute by mediation.

20. ARBITRATION
20.1 When such a dispute cannot be resolved by this means, if both Writer and Publisher/Client agree, each may appoint one representative to a three-member arbitration board.

20.2 The third member, who will chair the arbitration board, will be appointed by agreement of the first two members. If the two members cannot agree, the third party will be appointed by the court in accordance with provincial laws governing arbitration.

20.3 Neither the Writer nor an employee of the Publisher/Client may act as a representative or sit on the arbitration board.

21. DUTIES AND POWERS OF THE ARBITRATION BOARD
21.1 The arbitration board shall investigate and arbitrate only those disputes that are referred to it by the Writer and Publisher/Client, in accordance with subsection 20.1

21.2 The arbitration board shall rule on the dispute by a majority vote. That ruling shall be binding on both the Writer and the Publisher/Client and is not subject to appeal.

21.3 If arbitration involves costs, the arbitration board shall rule by majority vote on what percentage of costs will be paid by each party. That ruling shall be binding on both the Writer and the Publisher/Client and is not subject to appeal.

22. ACTION AT LAW STILL ALLOWED
22.1 This part does not prevent either the Writer or the Publisher/Client from pursuing an action in law provided an arbitration has not been initiated involving the same or a related dispute.

(continued on page 80)

AGREED AND CONFIRMED:

Signature of Writer

Date

Publisher/Client by (signature)

Date

Name:

Title:

Index

Web sites Cited
Copyright
Finance
Government
Legal
Other

Who Are We?

About the Contributors

To give you an idea of just who all this advice is coming from, here are some short bios of the writers who gave their two cents worth to this project:

Tracey Arial is a former PWAC president who has been a freelancer for eleven years. She is the author of three books: *I Volunteered: Canadian Vietnam Vets Remember*, and the *Ulysses Guides to Hiking in Ontario* and *Skiing and Shoeshowing in Ontario*. She is at work on a guidebook for the Trans Canada Trail Association.

Julie Barlow has freelanced for ten years and is a former Editor-in-Chief of English Language Projects for Montreal-based publisher Les Éditions Ma Carrière. She has also co-authored *Same Words, Different Language* (Piatkus, London) with international gender expert Barbara Annis and *Sixty Million Frenchman Can't Be Wrong* with Jean Benoit Nadeau. For more information, visit *www.sixtymillionfrenchmen.com*.

Ruth Bradley-St-Cyr worked in book publishing for thirteen years, at Stewart House, McGraw-Hill Ryerson, the United Church Publishing House, and several others. She has worked in local and student newspapers and was the publisher of *Growth Spurts*, an alternative parenting magazine. Ruth is currently the production manager of the *Canadian Journal of Development Studies*. She also just completed the book for a musical and is at work on a novel.

Ann Douglas, author of twenty-one books and an award-winning journalist and copywriter, has been a freelancer for fifteen years. A former PWAC president, she is also the founder of

Author Incubator (a coaching and mentoring service for authors) and both Author University and Freelancer University, two online communities for writers that will launch in mid-2004. Ann can be contacted via her Web site at *www.anndouglas.ca*.

Trudy Kelly Forsythe is a former special features writer for two New Brunswick daily newspapers and writes extensively for radio, print, and the Web in the Maritimes. She has been writing professionally for thirteen years.

Angie Gallop, a freelancer for eight years, is a Montreal-based writer and ESL teacher with a special interest in community development and urban life. She conducts a workshop, "What You Should Know Before You Go Freelance," for journalism schools and employment centres. She can be reached at *gallop@interlog.com*.

Barbara Florio Graham is a writer, teacher, broadcaster, and communications consultant. She has won awards for her non-fiction, humour, and poetry and is the author of *Five Fast Steps to Better Writing* and *Five Fast Steps to Low-Cost Publicity*. Barbara's company is named after her cat, Simon Teakettle, who "co-wrote" with her, a compilation of cat and human humour called *Musings/Mewsings*. You can find her at *www.simonteakettle.com*.

Hélèna Katz is an award-winning journalist who has freelanced since 1993. Her work has appeared in a variety of magazines both in Canada and the US and she has given marketing workshops for freelancers in Ottawa, Victoria, Montreal, and the Maritimes. She can be reached at *katzcomm@look.ca*.

Mark Kearney is an award-winning journalist and writing instructor at the University of Western Ontario and Lambton College. He is the co-author, with Randy Ray, of six books of Canadiana. He has been a writer for twenty-six years and a full-time freelancer since 1989. You can find out more at *www.triviaguys.com*.

Heather Kent is a former physiotherapist who has been a freelance medical writer since 1995. Her work has appeared in Canadian consumer magazines and she is a regular contributor of news, features, and research reviews to the *Canadian Medical Association Journal*. She also works with SportMedBC as an editorial consultant and writer.

Dale D. Kerr, M.Eng., P.Eng., has been providing freelance writing and editing services for over ten years through her company, Kerr Associates Technology Transfer, of Sutton, Ontario. She writes extensively for architecture and engineering magazines and trade journals, and specializes in writing concise, easy-to-read summaries of government research reports. Dale is also a partner, with her husband, in an engineering firm based in Newmarket, Ontario.

Kathe Lieber, a former PWAC president, has been a happy, productive freelancer since 1982. In 1988, she travelled to the former USSR with a delegation of Canadian journalists. She writes on a variety of topics, including fundraising, health, education, parenting, and history, producing newsletters and annual reports as well as editing and translation. She is the co-author of *Montreal: The International City*.

Paul Lima has been a freelancer for almost fifteen years. A regular contributor to the *National Post's FP Business Edge* section and many other periodicals, he specializes in technology and small business issues. Paul also teaches writing workshops and can be reached through his Web site at *www.paullima.com*.

Denyse O'Leary is a Toronto-based freelance writer and the author of the award-winning *Faith@Science* (Winnipeg: J. Gordon Shillingford, 2001). Her forthcoming book, *By Design or By Chance?: The Growing Controversy Over the Origin of Life in the Universe* (Castle Quay Books, Oakville, Spring 2004) has already received acclaim. You can find out more at *www.designorchance.com*

Michael OReilly, PWAC president in 2003/2004, is a print and radio journalist who has been a full-time freelancer for the past decade. He has also edited small and medium-sized newspapers as well as a national canoeing/kayaking magazine. Find out more at *www.helplink.com*.

Gil Parker has been freelancing for fourteen years. His expertise includes engineering consulting, energy technology, and international trading. Over the past fourteen years, he has written for many magazines including *Explore, Beaver, Monday Magazine,* and *Above & Beyond*. He also edited *Bridging the Pacific* and is the author of *Aware of the Mountain: Mountaineering as Yoga*. He is working on a book about Russia.

Heather Pengelley has freelanced for over 20 years, writing about everything from business to travel. She writes for periodicals, such as *The Gazette, Reader's Digest* and *Trade & Commerce*. As a medical writer, she works on video scripts, symposium reports, continuing medical education courses and slide presentations. She teaches business communications and technical writing at Concordia University in Montreal.

Tim Perrin has freelanced since 1967 and is an author of five books, a former broadcaster and later, a lawyer with a special interest in the legal problems of writers. He is now a full-time writer, editor, and teacher. His seminars are offered online at *www.writingschool.com*.

Alex Roslin is a Montreal writer and researcher for CBC-TV's *Disclosure*. He is working on a book about how police departments protect officers who abuse their spouses. He has been a freelancer for nine years.

Deborah Schoen is a freelance researcher and writer specializing in public health and environmental sciences. In addition to magazine writing, she has prepared literature reviews, symposium proceedings, educational materials, and public outreach documents for provincial, federal, and international health and environmental agencies. She has been a freelancer for seven years.

WHO ARE WE?

W.D. Valgardson, is a Governor General's Award nominee who has published thirteen books, written a dozen plays, and has had five movies adapted from his stories. He is also Chair of the writing department at the University of Victoria and a former public school teacher.

Liz Warwick, a freelance writer for the past eight years, has contributed to many publications including *Maclean's*, *Homemaker's*, *Applied Arts Magazine*, and *The Gazette*. She has also worked as a CBC researcher, contributed to the Biotech Career Guide and written for the Urban Issues Program of the Samuel and Saidye Bronfman Family Foundation. She lives in Montreal, writing for a variety of publications as well as corporate clients.

Stephanie Whittaker came to freelancing after a 12-year career as a newspaper journalist – during which she was a reporter, columnist, bureau chief and ombudsman. Since then she has been freelancing for nine years. She writes weekly for *The Gazette* and periodically for *Canadian House & Home*, *Canadian Gardening*, *Flare* and *Canadian Living*. Her newspaper features are published in CanWest newspapers across Canada.

Bruce Wilson is a medical writer and consultant who writes for both the lay and medical press. Before he started his writing career he was a medical researcher, health educator, taxi driver, and logger, among several other occupations. He has also been a health columnist for *The Georgia Straight* and managing editor for the Medical Education Network of Canada. In addition to chairing PWAC's Mediation Committee, he is also a member in good standing with the American Medical Writers Association. Her has been a full-time freelancer since 1995.

Mark Zuehlke, a former PWAC president, has been a freelancer for over twenty years and has written or co-written more than seventeen books. His latest work includes military history books focusing on the experiences of Canadians at war and an award-winning mystery series starring reluctant hero, remittance man, and coroner Elias McCann.

89

What is PWAC?

The Periodical Writers Association of Canada

In 1976, a group of freelance writers started meeting to share information and stories about writing for Canada's magazines and newspapers. They quickly realized that when writers worked together – by, for example, talking about rates they were being paid – they could more effectively protect their interests and strengthen the writing community as a whole. From those meetings grew PWAC, an organization that now serves over 500 freelance writers across Canada.

Today, PWAC's goals are:

- To develop and maintain professional standards in editor-writer relationships.
- To encourage higher industry standards and fees for all types of freelance writing.
- To offset the isolation so commonly felt among freelance writers by providing networking opportunities, regular meetings, and the chance to share their experiences.
- To provide professional development workshops and materials for members across the country to explore current issues and trends within the industry.
- To provide information on issues, trends, and new technology that is of interest to writers.
- To mediate grievances between writers and editors.
- To work actively for the survival of periodical writing in a highly competitive communications environment.
- To lobby for freedom of the press and freedom of expression in Canada.

To become a member of PWAC, please consult our Web site for more information: *www.pwac.ca*.